7 JOB LANDING STEPS TO FIND A ROLE THAT MAKES YOU HAPPY

STOP SEARCHING. START LANDING!

LISA RANGEL

COPYRIGHT © 2023 Chameleon Resumes LLC

This document is intended for private, individual use only by the individual purchasing the document. Transmission, distribution, duplication or public use by any means (electronic, mechanical, recording, photocopying or otherwise) is prohibited without express written consent from Chameleon Resumes.

ISBN: 978-1-7333176-7-2

DISCLAIMER: While the author has used her best efforts in preparing and producing this ebook, she makes no guarantees, representations or warranties with the respect to the accuracy or completeness of the contents of this book and specifically disclaim any implied warranties for sale for fitness for a particular purpose. No warranty may be created or extended through affiliate or marketing partnerships in print or online sales and marketing materials. The advice and strategies contained herein are the opinions and based off client experiences of the author and may not be suitable for your situation. You should consult with a proper professional where appropriate. The author shall not be liable for any loss of profit, income or commercial damages, including but not limited to special, incidental, consequential or any other damage.

CONTENTS

Introduction: A New Beginning	v
Step 1: Define the Job You Want	1
Step 2: Evaluate Your Resume	10
Step 3: How Does Your LinkedIn Profile Measure Up?	21
Step 4: Create a Powerful Resume & LinkedIn Profile	33
Step 5: Create Effective Cover Letters & Career Communications	45
Step 6: Design & Execute Your Job Landing Plan	51
Step 7: Master the Interview Mindset to Land the Job	70
Conclusion	125
Next Steps	127
Appendix 1	129
Appendix 2	147
About the Author	149
Also by Lisa Rangel	151

INTRODUCTION: A NEW BEGINNING

Congratulations on your new beginning!

You have just taken the crucial first step to landing your ideal job. Getting started is always the hardest part—so keep the momentum going as you take the steps you need to take. This process is not for the faint of heart, so I commend you for taking action that will help you get to your goal.

But "find my dream job" is a difficult thing to aim for. Where to start? What to do first, and next? How to do it? It can feel extremely overwhelming when you know where you're going, but not how you're going to get there.

This book will show you the way.

The first step of the process is to define where you want to go. Which means you need to define what your ideal job will look like, so you can then develop the resume, job search tactics, and interview strategy to land that position. We must begin with the end in mind.

Deep down inside, do you love what you do, but just do not want to do it with the company you are currently with? If that's the case, we can focus on showcasing your expertise so it's attractive to competitors, associations, vendors, affiliates, and clients within your industry.

Or do you dream of turning one of your passions into a sustainable career? Maybe you can stay in your existing field to fulfill your passion. Or perhaps you'll need to pursue that passion outside your existing expertise. Many people would love to find work that's both intrinsically rewarding and financially sustainable.

Turning your dream into reality is no easy feat in up or down economies. But it is very much possible, if you're willing to do the work and take action.

Let's start at the beginning, with step 1—and define the job you want, then develop the mindset you need to get it.

STEP 1: DEFINE THE JOB YOU WANT
& DEVELOP THE MINDSET TO GET IT

It is 100% possible to turn your passion into a career—or integrate your passion into your career. Let's look at 4 ways to do this.

1. EXPLORING CORPORATE WORK AT COMPANIES THAT INSPIRE YOU

Let's say you have a talent for digital marketing, social media management, and email marketing, and want to leave your traditional corporate marketing job in pursuit of a role with a funky, progressive startup that serves small and mid-sized businesses. You can use the LinkedIn Company Search function to locate boutique marketing firms.

You can conduct a LinkedIn search on "digital marketing" or "social media management" to identify jobs, companies, and connections affiliated with digital marketing. Look at related skills in this section to identify other areas to pursue. For example, when looking at related skills for "digital marketing", you'll find that mobile marketing, digital strategy, or online lead generation are other fields you can incorporate into your job search.

You may realize you have a more marketable skill set than the one you initially identified—or that you have a stronger interest in another area with skills that can be easily cultivated.

2. NON-PROFIT AND VOLUNTEER OPPORTUNITIES

Many job seekers have made the shift from performing a function in a corporate role, such as an accounting position, to a similar position supporting a cause dear to their hearts. Accounting is crucial in non-profits and for-profits, so job seekers can market their skills to the company whose cause inspires them.

Another possibility, if you can't find the paid role you want, is to first volunteer your skills—which could lead to a paid position, should one become available.

Have you always wanted to work for a company that supports cancer research? Do you want to help children with autism?

First, volunteer your skills for a cause you're passionate about to get your foot in the door. If you're an accountant, you can work for a cancer research non-profit in the accounting and finance department. Search for Controllers and CFOs of local and national cancer research fundraising organizations using search engines and LinkedIn's People Search.

Do you have a gift for managing staff and identifying talent? Apply your human resources expertise to a membership development role within the non-profit cause that lights a spark within you. Using LinkedIn's Company search to identify target companies to approach is a good place to start.

3. HOBBIES

Love to run? Perhaps your corporate skill set would be of value to an organization that targets runners. Or you could develop a side business venture connected to running, since not all passions have to develop into full-time employment. In either case, begin by using LinkedIn Groups to find groups containing the term "running". You'll find groups associated with marathons, half-marathons, and countless other running enthusiast groups.

Review the backgrounds of group members for common points or connections. Do they work at companies that support an aspect of running, such as apparel, vacation tours, events, or sports advertising? Do they work at "regular" companies with active running groups? Use LinkedIn Groups to connect to these groups. You can then engage members who share your passion for running, so you can gain insight and make contacts that might lead to a job related to running.

4. CULTURE & WORLD TRAVEL

Have a passion for history? Want to see the world? Have you considered finding international opportunities in your current field? You can use search engines and the geography search option found on LinkedIn to identify people and companies in places you've always wanted to visit—especially those that employ people with your background and require the country's expertise you bring to the table.

Reach out to new contacts discovered through your research to learn more about working in these industries and geographic locations. You can determine which lifestyle and financial changes may be required to make this career shift. Perusing LinkedIn

Groups can help you further build your network and reach out to individuals who are already engaged in your area of interest.

EXPLORING COMPANIES AND FINDING CONTACTS WHO CAN BENEFIT FROM YOUR PASSION AND SKILL SET

You have now begun to identify organizations and connections that can help in your quest to land a career rooted in your passion. The next step is to make contact and conduct exploratory conversations with key individuals to learn all you can about transitioning to this area. Your exploratory questions and conversations should help you decide how to structure your new pursuit to fit your lifestyle and financial needs.

Here are a few steps you can take:

- **Follow your target companies** on LinkedIn and other social media platforms to learn as much as you can about the culture and nuances of the industry and organization. This information will help you make an informed approach at the right time.
- **Sign up for email newsletters** or blogs to receive updates about networking opportunities and trending topics on your area of passion. Entrench yourself in your area of passion to learn as much as you can about working in that industry from these sources.
- **Set up a communications strategy** outlining how often you will reach out to contacts within and outside your network to further your pursuit of new opportunities. Track how many contacts you will reach out to per week via email, phone, and in-person meetings to help

you stay grounded and avoid the risk of over- or under-estimating your efforts.
- **Open your mind** to how this new pursuit might manifest itself—it may not lead to a job right off the bat. Consider consulting assignments, entrepreneurial ventures, and volunteer opportunities if the desired job doesn't appear.
- When approaching companies, **outline in a cover letter how your passion qualifies you for consideration.** Help the reader see how your skill set is transferrable to this new area that inspires you. Keep it concise, to the point, and focused on what you can bring to the organization.

Don't get discouraged. Stay the course. Anticipate that your desire to transition into work that inspires you may not at first be welcomed by employers, friends, or family. Focus on improving your qualifications and remember to network to spread the message of your dream. You only need one person to believe in you, to give you the chance to work at what you love. Don't give up on your passion or yourself.

GETTING IN THE RIGHT MINDSET TO GET JOB SEARCH RESULTS FAST

The proper mindset for conducting an effective job search and getting results from your efforts is to use the most contemporary tactics, embrace the tools available to you as a job seeker in today's employment landscape, and simply connect with people. Do not let technology rule your search, but use it to enhance your relationship-building activities to gain traction for the jobs that are right for you.

Submitting to job postings without talking to people is not an effective search strategy. When this limited approach does not work for certain experienced job seekers, they often blame the lack of response on age, race, sex, ethnicity, or other characteristics they have no control over—and those characteristics are probably not the issue. Limiting your actions to *only* submitting to job search postings is the least effective job search strategy out there. A deeper, more thoughtful approach will give you a much better chance to get the results you want.

Embrace technology to deepen your existing connections online and offline, and make new connections. Here are some tactics for you to employ and mindsets you can adopt as we go through the process:

- **Be able to communicate via technology**—email, social media, text, phone, and Zoom/video. Familiarize yourself with how to communicate using the various technologies available to you. You may be familiar with these already, which is fabulous. But if you aren't, then get on it. When a 22-year-old is asked to Zoom/Skype/Teams for a discussion and doesn't know how to do it, the interviewer may think the applicant is not that smart or really inexperienced. When a 40-year-old+ applicant doesn't know how to Zoom/Skype/Teams, the assumption is they are out of touch with technology and do not understand today's world. Don't give anyone a reason to make their negative assumptions (which are typically wrong) come to life.
- **Study online marketing concepts** to understand how your communications can capture attention in an online world. Understand the importance of email

subject lines, the best time of day to email, etc. This will help you communicate more effectively using technology. Understanding the nuances of subject lines, character limits (social media), and the best time of day to send a message can help your messages be better received by the reader and, frankly, make you look like you "get it."

- **Don't insist on in-person meetings, phone calls, or <gasp> faxing items** if the hiring manager requests email or scanning. And do not ask to fax over a resume. If they communicate with you via email, then communicate via email and get good at it fast! Saying, "If I can just get in front of them!" or "If I can just talk on the phone with a human, I know I can make an impression," will not help you or get you an interview. **Speak to people in the medium in which they speak.** I've seen clients get traction with a contact who is constantly on social media—after emailing them with no response. Don't get me wrong, the phone can work also... but if you've called several times and are not reaching the person, see what other mediums they communicate in and go there. If they're speaking in email, then speak via email as best you can. Try all different mediums, not just the ones you're familiar with.
- **Embrace and master the online job application.** Do not begrudge it or fight it. It is here to stay, like mobile phones. It's not going anywhere... I challenge you to embrace and master what you fear, whether that be online applications, the interview question you hope they don't ask, etc.

- **Practice phone, Zoom/Skype/Teams, and video interviewing** to ensure you are most effective when it's most important. If you're nervous about using technology for interviews, practice with a friend or a coach, so the first time you try it is not on the interview itself. The real interviews should not be practice sessions for you if you're not naturally comfortable with new technology. We'll address this more fully in the interview portion of this book, but initial phone screens can happen during job search activities, so be prepared.
- **Communicate concisely and clearly**—no long cover letter manifestos. Contemporary cover letters are short and concise. They must not be a lengthy regurgitation of your resume history. Use the cover letter to sum up in three or four bullet points the skills and expertise that make you the right person for the job. Sandwich these with a brief opening paragraph stating the position you're applying for and a closing paragraph thanking the reader for their time. That's the basic structure. Long manifesto cover letters are a thing of the past. Keep that in mind as you write your next cover letter.

MAKE SOCIAL MEDIA SOCIAL

Use social media, but don't get lost in it. Use it with a purpose—to generate new and relevant contacts whom you eventually speak to offline. There are ways to do this successfully for the introvert and the extrovert, but essentially making social media social is about taking the connections you make online and taking them offline in email, phone, or in-person conversations.

Look for leaders in your discipline or industry and start

following them. Then comment on their content and promote their wins by sharing their posts with your followers.

Another easy way to participate in the virtual conversations around you is to help others. Offer information when a virtual connection posts a question. Take part in social media chats related to your job or industry. Start with your interests and maybe you can find an opportunity to do what you already do within an industry that excites you.

- Call the social media contacts you follow
- Take part in chats (social media) and online live events
- Comment on blogs and status updates
- Promote your connections' wins
- Give information to help start a dialogue

The key is to embrace the technology available to you slowly, and be where hiring managers may be for your field.

STEP 2: EVALUATE YOUR RESUME
WHY YOU NEED A POWERFUL RESUME TO LAND AN INTERVIEW

In today's tough economy, employers often receive hundreds of resumes for each available position. A Powerful Resume is a results-driven tool you can use to ensure your qualifications stand out from the competition. Not only does it show your skills and experience in the best possible light, it's written and formatted to cut through the screening tools employers use to rule out most applicants. A Powerful Resume jumps to the top of the pile.

4 CHARACTERISTICS OF A POWERFUL RESUME

1. **A Powerful Resume communicates concisely.** Successful candidates format their resumes to present their strongest points in the top half of the document. The employer does not have to scroll to find them. They only need to scroll for specific details and

additional information, enabling them to see immediately that you're a suitable candidate for the role.
2. **A Powerful Resume uses results-driven formatting and language,** organized into clear sections, giving employers the information they want and need in an easily digestible format.
3. **A Powerful Resume design creates immediate impact.** In the sea of traditional, dated-looking resumes, a Powerful Resume uses a crisp, professional design for strong visual appeal.
4. **A Powerful Resume can successfully stand alone.** Even if separated from its cover letter, a Powerful Resume still conveys to the employer exactly which position the job seeker is pursuing.

FOUR REASONS EVERY JOB SEEKER NEEDS A BRANDED SUMMARY

A Powerful Resume will have a strong branded summary at the top. A branded summary encapsulates what you have done and what you can do for a prospective employer. Think of it as a tl;dr (too long; didn't read) section for employers to skim. Writing your branded summary in this format accomplishes four important tasks:

1. Shows the reader EXACTLY your area of strength or specialty at a glance.
2. It's loaded with relevant keyword phrases in natural language to improve searchability.
3. Conforms to how readers scan documents for information. People rarely take the time to read entire

documents. You keep the reader engaged to scroll and read more.
4. The topical items listed in the bullet section reinforce your areas of expertise to the reader, well before they read the entire resume.

How does your resume measure up?

A 36-POINT RESUME ASSESSMENT CHECKLIST

Whether you currently have a resume or are creating one from scratch, this 36-Point Resume Assessment Checklist will help you get your resume in top-notch shape.

Use this list with the Powerful Resume samples in Appendix 1 to create a Powerful Resume that will get employers' attention.

Getting Started

1. __Choose a contemporary font like Calibri or Arial Narrow for creative professions and a traditional font like Cambria or Garamond for conservative positions. Do not use ornate or script fonts. Fonts that vary too much from the accepted norms can leave negative impressions and may not be recognised by resume databases.

2. __Use a type size between 10 and 12-point for resume text. For section headings, use up to a 16-point size. Use 9 or 9.5-point type for firm descriptions. Never use a type size smaller than 9 or larger than 16—it must be easy to read.

3. __Use a layout and design that reflects the position and compensation you seek. This is your marketing document. Your

STEP 2: EVALUATE YOUR RESUME

resume's font, borders, and layout should properly organize and clearly present your information to convey the appropriate image.

Contact Information

4. ___Place your contact information at the top of the resume but not in the header. Resume databases and email previewers rarely pick up information in headers or footers. Include your physical address, personal email address, and cell phone number.

5. ___Include your social media links with your contact information. Share your LinkedIn Profile URL, Facebook page, and any relevant social media account under your name, address, phone number(s), and email address. Make sure the links support your professional purpose and are not personal.

6. ___If you went to a top school and/or a school with a robust alumni network, use your school's email address (yourname@schoolname.edu). It's the best tool for objective branding without appearing like a braggart. Otherwise, make sure your email address is neutral and professional.

Branded Summary Section

7. ___Remove any section titled "Objective" that states what you're looking for in your next role or company. Employers want to learn what value and skills you will bring to their organization—not what you're looking for in your next role.

8. ___Create a Summary section with a branded title or heading for yourself that relates to the job you're applying for—for example: Project Manager; Business Analyst; Versatile Office Manager;

Marketing Communications Specialist. Make it easy for the reader to position you in the context of their company. This will also help identify the job for which you are applying, even if your resume is separated from your cover letter. See The Branded Summary Section and the Powerful Resume Examples to see how you can do this.

9. __Under your branded heading, create a bulleted key word section using phrases, topics, and skills you derive from job ads for the position you're targeting. Resume databases and recruiters use key phrases to source candidates; this list will help them find you and will make sure you offer them exactly what they're asking for. See the Branded Resume Examples in Appendix 1 to see how you can do this.

10. __Use action verbs and nouns when writing your title and keyword section—like "profitable" and "optimized". Avoid subjective descriptions such as reliable, excellent, best, and cooperative.

Employment Section

11. __Save space on the first page—don't use the heading "Experience". This will be obvious to the reader. Later in your resume, use headings such as Skills, Interests, Education, Licenses, Certifications, Training/Professional Development, or Volunteer, because they make that information clear to the reader.

12. __All employment bullets need to start with an action-driven verb. Use the Action Verb List in Appendix 2 to help you create strong employment bullets. Do not list job description responsibilities or tasks. Do not use nouns to begin your bullets.

STEP 2: EVALUATE YOUR RESUME

Do not start with phrases like, "Duties included..." or "Responsible for", as this does not conjure an image of action, but a passive list of boring tasks.

13. ___Use present tense verbs for positions you currently hold and past tense verbs for all past positions. Do not use first person pronouns anywhere in the resume... ever.

14. ___Do your bullets demonstrate how you can solve problems experienced by the prospective company? Ask this question for each bullet on your resume. Review ads that describe the job you're seeking to ensure you customize your resume appropriately.

15. ___Include employment experience within the last 15-20 years. Do not cite jobs from over 15-20 years ago. Exceptions to this rule can be jobs that resulted in earning a professional certification (i.e. CPA), or jobs with a top-tier company that show exceptional caliber and depth of experience (i.e. early Microsoft or Fortune 100 experience). Other than these exceptions, it's better to leave off experience from over two decades ago.

16. ___Ensure your employment bullets cite measurable achievements. Show the results of your work using quantifiable references. Answer the question, "How do I know I did a good job?" with numbers for each bullet. Outline how you reduced expenses, increased revenue, optimized services, or streamlined a process.

Example: "Drove membership to highest level in organization's history" does not give a sense of scale. But "Drove membership from 50 to 75" or "Drove membership from 1,500 to 4,500", are two different experiences, despite both starting the sentence with "Drove membership…" The numbers give context to your achievements.

17. __Give a sense of size and scope to your previous and/or current employer.

Example: If you list, "Managed financials for a start-up division of this progressive Fortune 500 firm" there is no sense of the size of the budget. It is better to write the bullet as, "Managed the $400,000 budget for a start-up division of this progressive Fortune 500 firm." This gives a greater sense of the size and scope of the environment where you worked.

18. __Structure your promotions at one company under a single company heading. Do not show them as jobs under separate company headings. Using separate headings gives the impression that you had roles at different companies, when in actuality, you were promoted. Listing your progress under one heading shows your career progression at one company versus different companies. See the Powerful Resume Samples for how to do this.

19. __Accentuate the positive attributes in your background and de-emphasize the negative with placement and font treatment (bold, italics, and underlining).

Example: If you worked for elite companies, make the company names more prominent by listing them first. If you have relevant job titles but you're looking to switch industries, downplay the company names where you worked and emphasize the titles you held.

STEP 2: EVALUATE YOUR RESUME

20. __Do not emphasize your number of years of experience with phrases like, "Over 25+ years experience" or "Seasoned Executive". Instead, lead with measurable achievements showing where you made money, saved money, streamlined a process, and/or contributed to the company culture. Do not lead with your age... lead with your accomplishments.

Education Section

21. __Schooling should be at the bottom of your resume unless you graduated within the past 1-3 years from an area of study related to the work you're pursuing and it is a different field from your past/current work experience.

22. __Include your GPA if you graduated within the past 5 years and your GPA was above 3.0.

23. __If you graduated from school over 15 years ago, you do not need to include the year of graduation. Always include honors and honor societies from universities/colleges.

24. __Once you obtain your Bachelor's degree, don't list your Associate's degree.

Additional Sections

25. __When listing volunteer or professional affiliations, use the same parameters as listing an employer. Give yourself an appropriate title like "Membership Coordinator" or "Financial Manager" instead of "Volunteer". If you have this experience listed in a section called "Volunteer", it is obvious you are/were a volunteer. Write achievement-driven bullets outlining your

accomplishments, such as any fundraising goals you met, membership increases, budgets managed, programs administered, groups coordinated, and other crucial functions that made a positive difference.

26. __Remove any clubs or associations that relate to religious, political, or controversial issues.

27. __Ensure any software skills you list are current and relevant to today's marketplace.

28. __If you have them, list language skills other than English on your resume. If you're bilingual, do not list English as one of your languages for domestic positions—it's implied. If the bilingual skills are highly pertinent to the position you're applying for, consider including it in the branded summary at the top of the resume.

29. __Do not add any references to your resume and remove the "References Available Upon Request" statement at the bottom. Employers understand references will be provided if asked during the interview process, so don't waste space stating the obvious.

30. __Include social media links to your profiles if they're relevant and appropriate for hiring managers to see. Sharing social media links will show you're up to speed on current practices used by employees today.

Overall Analysis & Review

31. __If you have a 2+ page resume, ask yourself, "Am I keeping the reader interested in 5-10 second increments to ensure they read

STEP 2: EVALUATE YOUR RESUME

the subsequent pages?" Just because you send a two- or three-page resume does not mean the recipient will read it.

32. __Use a contemporary layout (see samples in Appendix 1) but do not insert graphics, text boxes, or tables into your resume. Resume databases cannot read them easily. Use the borders/shading function in MS Word to create simple design elements without inserting lines or complex graphical components.

33. __Test your resume online and on paper. Print it out and see that it looks as you expected. Open the document to view it on your computer screen—is the formatting as you expected? Make sure there are no odd page breaks.

34. __Put your name, contact information (email and/or phone number only) and page number on subsequent pages and addenda of your resume.

35. __Can people read your resume on most commonly used smartphone devices and within resume databases? This is worth exploring since most people do not work in front of a PC all day anymore. To create a text-only resume (called an ASCII Resume) for online job applications that populate resume databases, save your resume as a .txt file.

36. __Put your bullets to the test:

- Are they easy to understand?
- If you say the bullet phase aloud, does it make sense?
- Would the bullets make sense to someone outside your industry?

. . .

Now you've finished auditing your resume, you can take the next step to rebuild any sections of your resume—or start over—that need more work. This will ensure you have the best Powerful Resume to showcase your skills effectively. Use the Powerful Resume Format, the Action Verb Guide, and Resume Samples to get you started!

STEP 3: HOW DOES YOUR LINKEDIN PROFILE MEASURE UP?

A 22-POINT ASSESSMENT CHECKLIST

Your LinkedIn profile is a crucial tool in your job search, and will be one of the first things a recruiter or potential employer looks at. As the cliché goes, you only get one chance to make a first impression—so make sure your LinkedIn profile measures up.

Use this 22-point checklist to complete the relevant sections of your LinkedIn profile, and follow the guidance to ensure your profile is in alignment with your resume, to give yourself the best chance of success.

1. Get your name in lights

Enter your name as you want people to use it. You can use the former name function, if you changed your name over the course of your career, and want recruiters to find you under your former name, too. You can choose who can see your former name—make sure it's visible to the right people for optimum reach for your goals.

2. Make the most of your tagline

Optimizing your tagline with keywords and phrases is very important for an effective LinkedIn Profile. In your tagline, also known as your headline, use the keywords, descriptors, and deliverables the relevant hiring managers and recruiters will search for. Do not let your tagline default to your current job title; instead, use this area to give the reader a snapshot of your skills and personality, motivating them to click on your profile link to read further. Hiring managers really do use these keywords to find people like you! Look at your target job descriptions and your current job description to get an idea of the best keywords to show readers what you're looking for and what you've done.

3. Use a professional headshot photo

Whether you hire a professional photographer or use a do-it-yourself photo, choose your LinkedIn profile picture carefully—use a photo that is professional and appropriate for the type of industry you're in and the type of job for which you're applying.

Recruiters and hiring managers want to feel a personal connection with you as a candidate, which is why your photo is so important. LinkedIn recently increased the size of the photo and moved it to a more prominent position. Job seekers need to know that not having a picture, or possibly worse, having a poor picture front and center, is a serious detriment to their job search efforts.

Including a photo on your LinkedIn profile increases the chances of your profile being viewed by 40%. Invest in a professional picture or, at a minimum, choose a photo you already have—but make sure you're professionally attired, and the image is closely cropped. Choose a headshot that is free from blurs, other people, and background distractions—and don't use a group shot you've cropped yourself out of because it's almost always obvious.

4. Use a background photo for additional personal branding

You have the option to include a background photo to complement your profile photo for further branding and to give more information about who you are. You can choose an image (ensure you have the rights to use the photo) or use software (Canva is great for this) to create an image of a quote that embodies what you stand for... this is a great place to show your personal brand and promote the image you want to put out there. This image should be a .jpg, .gif, or .png file.

5. Claim a vanity URL

It's a lot easier to point people to your LinkedIn profile when you have a direct link with your name in it. LinkedIn allows you to customize your profile URL easily, and you should absolutely change it. Otherwise, you'll be stuck with a long, abstract, generic URL that will be difficult to include on your resume and/or business cards. Go to LinkedIn Help and search for "customizing your public profile URL" for instructions.

6. Include your contact information neatly in a contact information folder

Under the vanity URL and top third of your profile, you have the option to include a social media handle, three websites, a company web address, phone number, and email address (and more), all neatly placed in an address file at the lower right-hand corner of your intro box—alongside your LinkedIn URL. You can easily find contact information when you're working through your target list—and hiring managers can easily find your contact information when they want to get in touch with you.

7. Adjust your public profile settings

LinkedIn automatically sets profiles to be seen by the public. You can customize which sections are visible, and which are not in a search engine result. Review which sections you want included as it pertains to your profession and industry. Typically, you'll want all the sections visible; however, you may decide to choose a different strategy.

Allowing public visibility in some capacity allows your profile to show up in search results when someone searches for your name. And when someone clicks on your profile through that search engine result, the viewer will see what you make visible in your public profile.

Understanding the components of developing a robust LinkedIn Profile is a key piece of finding success in your job search using LinkedIn.

8. Create achievement-driven summary & experience sections

The summary section gives you 2,600 characters to showcase your achievements and key accomplishments. Fill it with examples of how you achieved specific results, rather than simply recapping your experience. You can also reference other parts of your profile here, to encourage readers to keep scrolling to where your work is more prominently displayed.

This is where you can build your brand. Your brand is not only what you want to project of yourself, but what your employers, coworkers, vendors, and clients know you for.

STEP 3: HOW DOES YOUR LINKEDIN PROFILE MEASURE UP?

Remove the fluff and clichés from your summary and, instead, pack it with action-driven information and language, letting your personality shine through for that prospective employer. Don't just tell someone you are results-driven—demonstrate it by citing results in your profile. Show the trait; don't just say you have it.

The first 40-50 characters are crucial—this is the place to make your best first impression, because these are the first characters shown on a LinkedIn profile. To read the remaining characters on a desktop, people have to click on your profile. Give them a reason to do so with concise, powerful writing.

Write your summary and check how it looks when strangers view your profile. Do the first 40-50 characters motivate the reader to click and read more? Using this gut-check evaluation, you can determine what to lead with to make your best first LinkedIn Profile impression. Here is a guide to developing achievement-driven statements for your summary and experience sections. For each task or claim you are making:

- Ask yourself, "How did I make money, save money, streamline a process, improve the outcome, or contribute to culture?"
- Another way to ask this question is, "How do I know I did a good job?" Then describe what it looked like.

These two questions will steer you away from job responsibility tasks in your profile and put you on the road to developing accomplishment-driven language in your profile.

9. Use keywords in summary & experience sections

Keywords are important throughout your profile, not just in your tagline. In your summary and experience sections, use words that will enable hiring managers to "find you" for your skills in a keyword search.

Quick tip: cut and paste a job description into a word cloud function, such as wordle.net, to identify keywords and acronyms to include in your profile. Then incorporate these keywords into your summary and experience sections to improve your profile optimization. Then use these keywords to develop the skills section. Use descriptor words that share your abilities, subject expertise, and skill sets as often as possible, especially in your summary and experience sections.

10. Showcase your work

Several sections in your profile allow you to showcase your work and professional credentials and demonstrate your personality. All these sections add depth to your overall brand.

For example, use the Project Section to showcase work pertinent to your profession. Be sure you have permission to use this material publicly on your profile. This is great for copywriters, graphic artists, conference speakers, and corporate trainers, as an example. What you include here helps you stand out from other candidates.

Include relevant information in each of these sections, such as Publications, Projects, Courses, Volunteer Experience, and so on. Upload applicable white papers, media, presentations, and videos. Ensure that what you include reinforces your personal brand and the job you're looking for.

11. Complete all sections, including education, certifications & interests

The more complete your profile, the higher you'll appear in

STEP 3: HOW DOES YOUR LINKEDIN PROFILE MEASURE UP?

search results when your network looks for people like you. Be sure to complete all sections, including education, certifications, and interests, and the other section options you have.

When you're deciding what to include in each section, be conscious of the overall impact it will have on your personal brand. Include details that help enhance your brand and strengthen your profile—always keeping in mind the type of role you're looking for.

Do you know multiple languages, for example?

Have you received honours and awards?

Do you have patents to promote to the scientific or consumer goods community?

These details could certainly help you rise above the competition, so show them off.

12. Embed interesting media elements to keep the reader engaged

If you want to make your profile extra engaging to keep the reader scrolling, add media such as documents, video, images, and audio. This can transform your profile into an online portfolio.

Reference these works in your summary, so they motivate the reader to keep scrolling for the details. You can easily embed these links into your summary, work experience, education, project, and other sections.

As with everything else, make sure the media you choose supports your brand and reinforces your image positively.

13. Choose the right skills

The skills section allows potential employers to see at a glance the distinct skill sets you want to be known for. You can choose up to 50—but choose carefully. Remember your specialisation and focus only on the skills that make the most sense for your profile and the roles you're seeking. Check the job descriptions you are applying to for guidance on which keywords and phrases to include.

14. Get recommendations

Having colleagues, managers, clients, vendors, mentors, and others provide a recommendation about your work and capabilities is the best kind of social proof you can get on LinkedIn. Reach out to your connections and ask them to provide a recommendation. The more qualitative the recommendation, the better.

Be sure to approve and include the recommendations on your profile. Don't feel obligated to return the favor unless you have value to add by discussing your experience working with that person. But if you can add value to someone else's profile by commenting on your experience as co-workers, manager or subordinate, client, or vendor, please do so. Offering qualitative recommendations and receiving qualitative recommendation is key, but they do not need to be reciprocal.

15. Don't forget the endorsements

Endorsements get a bad rap because they are easy to give out and you might get endorsed for skills you do not want to showcase or may not even have. Have no fear. You have complete control over what skills get endorsed and the order they're shown—you do this when you choose the skills you want to showcase.

When you choose the right skills, your connections will provide endorsements for those skills. Keep the most relevant

STEP 3: HOW DOES YOUR LINKEDIN PROFILE MEASURE UP?

endorsements only; it's OK to delete endorsements for skills not relating to what you want to be found or recruited for.

LinkedIn endorsements are important, regardless of what people might think about them being too easy to get or diluting your recommendations.

You can choose to get notified when you someone endorses you, so you can thank your endorser. This is a great way to network and an opportunity to open up a dialogue with someone who may help you find the job you're looking for.

16. Rearrange sections to showcase your best self

Did you know you can rearrange the sections of your profile to suit what you deem most important and show you in the best light?

To do this, look for the icon in the upper right-hand corner of each section called "move LinkedIn sections." Then arrange your sections according to what's most important to your target audience. For job seekers, this is a potential employer.

17. Choose whether to include personal details

For US job seekers, you don't have to include personal details. For those seeking positions outside the US, it's often customary to include birth date and marital status. Evaluate your goals and decide if you want to include these pieces of information on your profile.

18. Align your profile data to your resume information

In most job application scenarios, hiring managers will visit your LinkedIn profile after they review your resume. It's important that your resume and LinkedIn profile are aligned with accurate information across both mediums.

Everything needs to match—it doesn't have to be word-for-word, but your dates, titles, information, skills, and so on need to agree. If they're not, it can leave employers questioning your attention to detail or even trustworthiness, and thwart your job search process.

19. Your LinkedIn profile should be mobile friendly

Fifty-seven percent of LinkedIn users use the LinkedIn Mobile app. It's true that the desktop version and mobile apps include the same profile information, but the layout and functionality are different, so there are a few things to pay extra attention to.

For example, pay attention to the first 40-50 characters of your Tagline and the same in your LinkedIn Profile Summary.

To know for certain how your profile appears on a mobile device, check it out on your own phone.

20. Activity and engagement are important

Profile engagement has immense value to the LinkedIn algorithm. Activity level is prominently showcased on your LinkedIn profile and is valued by LinkedIn. Taking part in groups, posting status updates, commenting on others' posts, and liking content shared by connections and group members are just a handful of ways to engage with others and share information with your connections. When someone looks at your profile, they can see how active (or not so active) you've been on LinkedIn and how often you've posted or shared relevant information. Staying current and active in your profile is as important as ever!

Update your status regularly so your network can see what

you're doing and you can stay on top of your network's mind. Status updates can be as simple as a link to an article you found interesting, information about an event you're attending, or a presentation you're giving.

You can encourage engagement by posing a question to your network or helping another LinkedIn member by answering their question. If you reach out to engage your network, this is how to get engagement in return.

Remember, having a robust LinkedIn profile is only one piece of the "getting more views on your profile" puzzle. Once you've completed your profile is completed, starting and joining conversations with others is key to getting profile views. Be active and consistent in your groups and with your connections and you'll see your profile views increase.

21. Update your connections

LinkedIn gives you a powerful tool to expand your network: once a month, update the contacts in your LinkedIn connections.

Go to My Network, and click on Connections, then click on the star wheel to the right to access a widget that allows you to add your Gmail contacts or import contact files so you can invite them to connect on LinkedIn.

Alternatively, under My Network, you can choose "Add Contacts" and LinkedIn lets you add individuals one-by-one or choose your email provider to sync your contacts with your profile connections.

22. Complete your profile 100%

When your profile is complete, it will show in LinkedIn search results of your networks. As a job seeker, this is paramount for being found by recruiters. Follow the prompts to complete your profile.

Do you have a gap or are you currently not employed? Here are creative, yet accurate, ways to give yourself a current employer section (one checklist item that contributes to a 100% complete profile) or account for gaps on your profile:

www.chameleonresumes.com/unemployed-suggestions-powerful-executive-linkedin-profile

Developing a robust LinkedIn Profile is a key piece a successful job search using LinkedIn. Implementing and adhering to these checklist items will give you a keyword-optimized, achievement-laden profile that, when combined with view-building activities, will increase the chances hiring managers will find you (and of you finding hiring managers) for the right job.

STEP 4: CREATE A POWERFUL RESUME & LINKEDIN PROFILE

BUILD YOUR RESUME & LINKEDIN PROFILE SECTIONS TO LAND INTERVIEWS

In this chapter, you'll start your Powerful Resume and LinkedIn Profile by following a step-by-step template. This will guide you in organizing and phrasing your current and past employment experiences, as well as your education, certifications, training, technical skills, and community volunteer activities—the customary sections of a resume and LinkedIn profile. It is important these documents have a message that aligns with the target job you seek.

After you have completed these sections, we will focus on the first item that appears on your resume: the summary. We do it in this order because the summary draws from the information you develop as you write the rest of your resume.

Be sure to check out the section titled "How to Phrase It Right—A Guide to Challenging Situations". This section will show you how to handle tricky situations like returning to work after a long period of absence from the workforce, shifting careers, being promoted from within a company, and other common life events.

EMPLOYMENT SECTION—FOR RESUME OR PROFILE

For each position you have held, include information using the following format of type, bold, underline, etc. Use other combinations to highlight different aspects of your experience:

COMPANY NAME, City/State **Dates Worked To – From**
Use this line to describe the business of the firm, citing revenues, staff size, and locations to give the reader context of your experience.
<u>Job Title</u>

- Cite your top three to five achievements in this job relating to how you may have increased revenues, reduced expenses, optimized services, or streamlined a process.
- Reference the crucial responsibilities you performed. Outline the size and scope of your results, which levels, with whom you interfaced inside or outside the company, and/or who you reported to if the position was relevant to what you're pursuing next.
- Answer the questions posed by potential employers, "How have you solved my problem?" or "How can you improve my organization?" by outlining how you've done this for your current and past employers.
- Start each bullet with an action verb. Do not start bullets with nouns or passive phrases such as: 'Responsible for', 'Duties included' or 'Liaison between'. See the following Action Verb Guide for ideas.
- For each bullet, add size and scope of the environment to place your achievements and responsibilities in their

STEP 4: CREATE A POWERFUL RESUME & LINKEDIN PROFILE

context. Quantify your achievements with measurable components wherever possible.
- When listing the dates of employment, be consistent in your formatting. Include month/year or just the year (depending on which best showcases your experience) but use the same format throughout.
- Look at the Powerful Resume Samples to learn how to handle multiple promotions or positions at the same company in the best way to showcase your progressive experience.

Repeat for each position going back 15-20 years. For positions you held over 20 years ago, either leave them off the resume entirely or include a catch-all statement at the end of the employment section, such as:

Prior staff and middle management roles at: McKinsey, IBM, and StarQuest.

ACTION VERBS

Use action verbs to tell your story with impact. They let you create impactful bullets that communicate clearly to hiring managers and resume readers exactly what you did and how you did it.

In Appendix 2, you'll find a list of action verbs pulled from the resumes and profiles created by Chameleon Resumes for our clients. Use them to help you create your own successful resume.

Remember: Use present tense verbs with current positions and past tense verbs for previous roles.

EDUCATION SECTION

After your work experience, add your education credentials.

This section should always follow the employment section unless (a) you graduated within the last year or (b) you're switching careers and your degree is relevant to the pursued position AND the degree was received within five years. In these two cases, it is appropriate to place the education section before the employment section.

Cite degrees in one of the following formats:

OPTION 1:

Rutgers University, Graduate School of Management, Newark, NJ — 2022
Masters of Business Administration – Concentration: Marketing

Douglass College, New Brunswick, NJ — 2018
Bachelors of Arts Degree - Major: Economics/Accounting - **GPA 3.84/4.00**

OPTION 2:

Notre Dame University, Notre Dame, IN — June 2019
Bachelor of Arts in Speech Communication

OPTION 3: If your degree was obtained over 15 years ago and/or you need to conserve resume space, use a one-line format.

Pennsylvania State University, University Park, PA - ***B.S. Business Administration***

Started but didn't finish your bachelor's or advanced degree? Here are some tips to formatting effectively:

- If you have an associate's degree and a bachelor's degree, only list the bachelor's degree.
- Include the amount of credits you have thus far if it is over half the credits needed.
- List that you are a Bachelor of Science Degree Candidate (or Master's Degree Candidate).

- List "Expected Completion 2023"—or whenever you expect to complete it, within 2-3 years.

OPTION 4:

Boston College, Boston, MA **Expected Date of Completion June 2022**
Bachelor of Arts Candidate: Major: Liberal Arts

TRAINING AND/OR CERTIFICATIONS SECTIONS

This should be separate from the Education section. You can combine each topic or list under separate headings, depending on the relevance, volume, and timeframe of each entry. Make sure any conferences and training seminars listed are relevant to advancing your career.

For certifications and training credentials, include the organization issuing the certification or training, as well as what you earned, and the year you got it.

Here are examples of how to format your certifications and training:

CERTIFICATION
Certified Public Accountant designation in NY State   2019

TRAINING & DEVELOPMENT
Miller Heiman, *Strategic & Conceptual Selling Courses*   Fall & Spring 2020
American Marketing Association, *Permission-based Marketing*   Spring 2021

SKILLS SECTION

This section is straightforward and typically refers to technical abilities. Technical resumes must clearly delineate between hardware, software, programming languages, operating systems, and web-based functions. For everyone else, it's imperative to show technical proficiency with common office systems and industry—or discipline-specific programs and client management systems (CRMs).

As far as formatting, the most effective way is to simply list them in a prose format separating each item with a comma. You can use column format, if space allows. Examples of this are:

TECHNICAL CAPABILITIES

Programming Languages: C++, PHP, Python, JavaScript
Databases & Database Programs: MySQL SQL Server, Oracle, Crystal Reports, Excel Macros, MS Access,
Hardware: Cisco IOS (routers, switches & firewalls), Network Monitoring tools, WAN, LAN, and iSCSI storage
Operating Systems: iOS, Windows, Linux, UNIX
Web Servers: Apache & IIS

SKILLS
InDesign, Adobe Photoshop, Adobe Illustrator, Acrobat, MS Office, Google Suite, Vertical Response (web-based email campaign application), social networking sites, PC and MAC platforms.

VOLUNTEER ACTIVITIES & PROFESSIONAL AFFILIATIONS SECTIONS

Format your volunteer and professional organization positions the same way as in the employment section, whenever possible. You can combine or separate them depending on how many and how relevant they are to the position for which you are applying.

Never simply call yourself a volunteer. If you organized members for an event or raised funds, consider giving yourself a title such as Event Coordinator or Fundraiser. For some of your volunteer and professional affiliation roles, you can outline what you achieved in bullets following the organization's name and title section.

Here are two examples:

STEP 4: CREATE A POWERFUL RESUME & LINKEDIN PROFILE

AMERICAN RED CROSS, Princeton, NJ – *Membership Coordinator*   2014- present
- Sat on the committee that planned and executed initiatives that increased membership 27% within six years.
- Compiled 10,000 prospective member lists and designed a permission-based email campaign that converted 11% of email recipients into new members.
- Received the "Volunteer of the Year" award in 2015

Professional Association of Electrical Engineers, Chicago, IL   June 2019 – present
Board Member (June 2009 – June 2010)
Participant Member (June 2010 – present)

Note: Only list clubs and associations that are not religious or political and do not represent controversial issues—unless you're applying to work for an organization where that cause or philosophy is its mission.

DESIGN YOUR BRANDED SUMMARY FOR IMMEDIATE VISUAL IMPACT

The unique strength of a Powerful Resume comes from its opening section—The Branded Summary. A Branded Summary encapsulates what you have done for previous employers and what you can do for a prospective employer. This highly focused section gets attention in resume databases and from recruiters who use keywords to search for potential applicants.

Now the body of your resume is complete (the employment, education and other sections), you can start working on this essential section. There are examples of how it should look on the following pages and in the Sample Resumes in Appendix 1.

Here are the 4 steps to take to create this impactful opener:

1. Assign yourself a **branded title** that reflects the job you're seeking and the experience you have already.
2. Write a **descriptive summary paragraph** under your branded title using the following structure:

- *First sentence* captures the value you'll bring to the employer.
- *Second sentence* demonstrates how you'll solve problems.
- *Third sentence* communicates soft skills that add value to the position for which you are applying.

3. Create a list of **bulleted skills and topical items** to place under your summary paragraph. These are:

- Noun-based (not verb-based) bullets to reinforce your qualifications in a concise format.
- Keyword phrases for optimum recruiter searching.
- Phrases derived from your past performance evaluations or from job ads.

4. Graphically frame the top and bottom of the section with a **border** that promotes the image you want to convey.

Three items you should NOT include in your Branded Summary section:

1. Do not use the title "Objective" ever.
2. Do not use first person ever.
3. Do not state what you're looking for, what skills you want to develop, what training you seek, or anything else you want. *This section is not about what you want. It is about what value, results, experience, and concrete skills you bring to the prospective employer.*

On the next page are three examples of effective Branded Summaries. See Appendix 1 for more examples.

STEP 4: CREATE A POWERFUL RESUME & LINKEDIN PROFILE

PROJECT MANAGER (PMP)

FINANCIAL SERVICES PROJECT MANAGER skilled at managing multi-faceted global projects by communicating clear mission and key objectives to cross-functional teams. Recognized for consistent success streamlining project workflows, meeting time deadlines and remaining within budget. Establish best practices for increased accountability, productivity, cost reduction, resource allocation and return on assets. Coach and mentor teams at all levels towards success, growth and fulfillment.

- Project Management and Reporting
- Global Business Process Improvements
- Quality Control & Process Re-engineering
- Data Gathering & Process Mapping
- Information Technology Needs Assessment
- Change Management & Performance Development
- Contract Negotiation & Facilitation
- Business Recovery & Contingency Planning

VICE PRESIDENT OF OPERATIONS

Solutions-driven Operations Vice President who qualitatively reduces expenses and enhances revenues through streamlining operations within cutting edge industries and competitive establishments. Establish priorities, leverage team skill sets and gain executive sponsorship to complete projects on time and within budget. Excellent process improvement, troubleshooting and communications skills honed at top firms.

- Cost & Expense Management
- Staffing Logistics & Hiring
- Client Quality Assurance
- Operational Policy & Procedures
- Internal Operational Audit
- Business Operations Analysis
- Project Management
- Training & Team Building
- Internal Communications

HEALTHCARE OFFICE MANAGER

Healthcare Office Manager of multi-doctor practices who streamlines office processes and develops productive staff to maximize profit margins. Consistently exceed company revenue goals through efficient expense management, effective operations training and creative marketing programs. Provide the highest level of patient service with accuracy and responsiveness. Experienced in opening and moving offices in new markets.

- Strategic Business Planning
- Forecasting, Budgeting & Accounting Operations
- Staff Training & Leadership Development
- Sales Development & Training
- Marketing, Advertising & Public Relations
- Executive Team Support

OUTLINING CHALLENGING SITUATIONS ON YOUR RESUME

The most important aim when presenting any sort of anomaly in your resume is to do so without distracting the reader from your qualifications.

It's crucial to present your information in such a way that it answers the question, "What did they do during that time?" without generating confusion. When the reader is confused by side questions, they're not focused on your experience. You want the reader to evaluate your qualifications and consider you for an interview, with anything non-standard being a non-issue. Here are suggested treatments for handling some common situations.

Gap in Your Resume

If you have a gap in your resume from over 10 years ago, minimize it by playing up your experience before and after the gap. Or, if it is a significant gap of over four years, consider adding a line that neutrally explains what took place during that period.

You can also populate this section with volunteer activities and other community leadership roles that you may have had during this time period. Examples are:

- Stay-At-Home Parent 2019-2022
- Fulltime Student 2020-2021
- Personal Leave 2019-2021—we can use this for caring for a sick parent or a personal medical leave. A simple phrase accounting for the time is all you need.
- Professional Research Sabbatical 2020-2021—be sure to have the activities and findings to back it up.

STEP 4: CREATE A POWERFUL RESUME & LINKEDIN PROFILE

Promoted Multiple Times at the Same Job

Congratulations!

The key here is to have your information visually represent the promotions.

The most common mistake job seekers make is to format the information so it looks like they had short jobs at separate companies—the complete opposite of what they intend to communicate!

Using the suggested format below will make it clear to the reader that you're on a progressive upward path in your career.

There are several additional examples of how to handle this situation in the Sample Resumes section.

BANANA REPUBLIC, New York, NY & Princeton, NJ   November 2018 – July 2022
Purchasing Manager *(October 2020 to July 2022)*
- Purchased, bid, and maintained inventory levels of all non-merchandise items for the company's 750 stores nationwide, 4 Distribution Centers, Corporate Operations Officer and the Canadian Home Office.

Assistant Manager *(November 2018 to October 2020)*
- Managed 24-employee staff and inventory for a $1.5 million dollar store in Central New Jersey.

Experience with a Company that was Renamed or Merged

These are common situations in today's marketplace.

The solution is to name the company you work/worked for and, in parentheses, give the current name of the company or the company with which it merged. Also include the year of the change.

Examples are:

MuleSoft *(now Salesforce, Inc. as of 2018),* Houston, TX   August 2013 – January 2020

AccountPros (merged with Accountants International in 2010), NY, NY   April 2008– February 2015

How to Handle a Layoff on Your Resume

Handling a layoff is more of a discussion strategy when preparing for an interview, and won't normally feature on your resume.

In most situations, you won't mention on your resume anything about how you left a position, unless it's related to a business activity such as a merger, acquisition, or corporate relocation. If your layoff is a result of one of these business situations, you can outline it on your resume and have the reader infer why you're no longer there.

Here are some examples:

FLUIDCLICK INC. (acquired by Google in January 2018), New York, NY   2011 – 2018
Client Accounting Manage1
   ** *It is implied that this job seeker is probably no longer at this job due to the Google takeover*

Union Bank (merged with U.S Bank in February 2023), NY, NY   April 2017 – April 2023
   ** *It is implied that this person is no longer with Union Bank due to the merger with U.S.Bank*

In Appendix 1, you'll find examples of Powerful Resumes you can model when you create your own resume.

STEP 5: CREATE EFFECTIVE COVER LETTERS & CAREER COMMUNICATIONS

TODAY'S CONTEMPORARY COVER LETTER & CAREER COMMUNICATIONS

Writing a great cover letter specific to each job search application is a must in today's career marketplace. Using a one-size-fits-all, general cover letter for all your applications and communications is not an effective way to uniquely present yourself in a job search.

The following six cover letter tips will help you write a concise, impactful cover letter that will improve your chances of getting noticed and receiving that call for the coveted interview:

1. **Ensure your cover letter is short**—no more than a computer screen shot or a couple of scrolls on a smart phone. That's it! Hiring managers and associates read little more than that. If it's longer, you risk your letter getting skipped.
2. **Address your cover letter to an actual person!** Do not send it "To Whom It May Concern" or "Hiring Manager." Do the homework and research the best person to send your cover letter to.

3. **Tell the person you're emailing how you found them.** Most people instinctively think something like, "How did they get my name?" when receiving an unsolicited, yet personalized inquiry. Show early in the cover letter email how you found them to put them at immediate ease so they want to continue reading. Whether it was research on LinkedIn or your former co-worker that led you to reach out to this person, telling the recipient how your email landed in their inbox makes the person feel better.
4. **Be explicit about the job you're looking for**, whether it's an exploratory request, or you're submitting to a job posting. Do not leave it up to the hiring manager to decide which job you're applying for or where you may fit within their organization. If you do, your cover letter may get filed under "T" (Trash).
5. **Do not write your cover letter as a prose version of your resume.** Period. It shouldn't be a regurgitation of your resume. A cover letter should summarize the value you'll bring to the prospective organization and show how your background fills a need they have. Nothing will put your credentials in the "no" pile faster than a lengthy synopsis of your career history with no clues how your credentials benefit the hiring organization.
6. **Help the reader connect the dots** about why they should take action and call you for an interview or forward you to the right person to bring you in for a discussion. Use only 3-5 bullets to outline how you are a fit for the prospective position.

Finally, of course, end your letter with professional niceties:

STEP 5: CREATE EFFECTIVE COVER LETTERS & CAREER COMMU...

thank the person for their time and assertively offer to follow up to set up an interview time. Polite enthusiasm and humble persistence are never out of style and always stand out positively in today's marketplace.

Review the following samples to help you craft your own cover letters and communication documents:

SAMPLE GENERAL COVER LETTER

Dear _____,

Leading global clinical trials is what my experience demonstrates that I do best. I bring to each initiative the ability to collaborate as part of a cross-functional team to develop programs, identify and select investigational sites, manage CROs and vendors, and oversee execution of Phase 1 and 2 studies for oncology, hematology, and cardiology therapeutic areas. I am seeking a role as a Clinical Project Director and submit my credentials to you, outlining how my qualifications are relevant to the needs outlined in the job description.

Throughout my career, I have worked in a project management capacity for leading global pharmaceutical and biotechnology companies, including Johnson & Johnson, Merck, and Imclone. My academic background in social work has enabled me to contribute a unique perspective and passion for making a difference by leading efficient and effective clinical trials.

Most notably, I was selected to lead one of Merck's pivotal oncology trials. This $18 million, 13-global site, 176-patient Phase 2 program was instrumental in filing the Briomade45 compound for specific melanomas. I was involved in the development, vendor selection and CRO management, protocol establishment, data collection and analysis, and regulatory documentation.

In addition to monitoring project budgets, deliverables, and milestones, I have earned a reputation as a motivational leader and innovative problem solver. On many occasions, I restructured failing studies by revising plans, creating documents and tools, and improving communication that facilitated the attainment of project goals.

Currently, I am pursuing opportunities to work as part of a progressive, world-class organization that values passion, commitment, and goal focus. My team building and motivational leadership, cultural diversity, global business acumen, and project management skills are unsurpassed.

I would welcome the opportunity to discuss with you how I can facilitate the attainment of your business goals and objectives. I would like to arrange a time to speak. You can reach me at 451.555.0670 or firstname.lastname@gmail.com.

Sincerely, FirstName LastName

SAMPLE CAREER NETWORKING COVER LETTERS/EMAILS/SCRIPTS

Voice Mail Script for Approaching New Contact Directly (from LinkedIn or other sources)

"Hi Jack, this is FirstName LastName. I'm reaching out to you in the spirit of networking, <as we have a mutual contact in> or <as while researching, I see you may be able to assist me>. I am seeking your expertise, because I'm searching for a role to spearhead a finance analysis function needing specific expertise in performing research on potential acquisition targets and identifying the viable targets to pursue. I'm hoping you may know of someone or an organization that could benefit from my experience. I'm happy to forward my resume to outline my current experience and help trigger any ideas. If you can help me, I would be most grateful. You can reach me at 451.555.0670 or firstname.lastname@gmail.com. Again, Jack, thank you for any time and help you may be able to provide."

Email Content for Reaching Out to Corporate or Client Alumni

I hope this introductory email finds you well. I am reaching out to you in the spirit of networking, as we both worked at <employer name> in our careers. Currently, I am conducting a job search for a Supply Chain Management leadership role requiring specific expertise in designing solutions for hospitality and mixed-use properties, as that is what my long term and recent experience shows. Would you know of someone or an organization that could benefit from my experience? Thank you in advance for any help you may be able to provide with my search. You can reach me at 451.555.0670 or firstname.lastname@gmail.com or let me know of a convenient time to call you for a 10-minute discussion on the matter. Again, thank you for any help you may be able to offer.

Specific Job Follow-Up Email Content

I hope this email finds you well. I am reaching out to follow up regarding the Marketing Manager position you posted on the company website. I am excited by the responsibilities and challenges posted in the job description and look forward to discussing with you how I can produce results if hired for the role. I have attached my resume for your reference.

I can be available at your convenience to review how my qualifications exceed what you stipulate in the job posting. I can be reached at 451.555.0670 or firstname.lastname@gmail.com.

Thank you for your consideration and I look forward to hearing from you soon.

Call or email to network with or gain information from contact out of <Target Company Firm>

I am reaching out in the spirit of networking and I hope this email finds you well. I am interested in exploring opportunities with <Target Company Firm>. I see on LinkedIn that you used to work for them and I was hoping you might help me out and steer me in the right direction. I would really appreciate if you could spare a few minutes and help me out.

Thank you in advance for any help you may be able to provide. You can reach me at 451.555.0670 or firstname.lastname@gmail.com or let me know of a convenient time to call you for a 10 minute discussion on the matter. Again, thank you for any assistance you may be able to offer.

Now you have your goals, your resume, your cover letter, and your LinkedIn profile ready—it's time to make a Job Landing Plan.

STEP 6: DESIGN & EXECUTE YOUR JOB LANDING PLAN
WEEKLY JOB SEARCH ACTIVITIES & HOW TO DO THEM

With a methodical plan, you'll keep a healthy mindset and find the position you need. If everything seems overwhelming, don't look at the entire process—just start by taking one action. That action will build on itself as you take further action from momentum you create.

Your broad plan may look like this:

1. Set activity metrics so you know what to do each week—here are a few examples of what to track:

- How many new networking contacts per week will you find and approach?
- How many people from your existing contact list will you contact—by phone or by email?
- How many new jobs will you apply to each week minimum?
- How many new companies will you find to target each week?

- How many new leads from these do you want to find each week?
- What about networking events? Lead meetings?
- How many Exploratory Coffee Appointments and Calls will you aim to set up each month?
- Block out no more than 1-2 hours per week to look at job boards—most job boards should send you alerts. See the website list and Google page to learn how to set up alerts on these sites.

2. Track your overall goals for each activity in a spreadsheet, and record the activity you actually perform each week. This will give you a picture, as time progresses, of where your results are coming from and how you're spending your time.

3. Email or call new prospects for exploratory interviews and conversations to learn more about target companies and roles and robustly develop your contacts. Use this as a basis to approach new contacts.

COMPILE YOUR TARGET COMPANY LIST

Conducting your job search only through submitting your resume to job postings is a sure-fire way to generate no interview responses—and create havoc with your job search mindset. Take back control of your job search and contact companies directly. Here is how:

Develop a list of companies to target your search activity based on one/some/all of the following criteria. Initially, focus your list development on the top 4 items.

(1) Direct Industry

(2) Geography

STEP 6: DESIGN & EXECUTE YOUR JOB LANDING PLAN

(3) Support-Type Organizations

(4) Associations/Non-Profits that serve your industry/discipline

(5) Consider each firm's clients, competitors, former employees, current employers, and vendors

Other items that can define your search:

(6) Size (Fortune 500, Mid-Size, Small)

(7) Type (Start-Up, Growth Stage, Established)

(8) Location suitable for a spouse's career

(9) School options for family

(10) Cost of Living versus Average Regional Compensation

Consider the following Websites to find target companies (some free, some charge a fee):

- www.DNB.com
- www.money.cnn.com—Fortune Lists
- www.forbes.com/lists
- www.inc.com—Lists

Within each company, search for the name(s) of the appropriate hiring managers (think of likely titles for a prospective boss) and/or the human resources manager as a secondary contact point. For each name you find, use a spreadsheet to capture the following minimum information:

- Contact Name
- Contact Title
- Company Name
- Email Address
- Phone Number
- Office Location
- Source Found
- Comments

Check out this blog post:
How to Build a List of Target Companies for Your Job Search
https://premium.linkedin.com/content/premium/global/en_us/index/jobsearch/resources/get-connected/how-to-build-a-list-of-target-companies

And this article:
19 Ways to Build your Target Company List http://chameleonresumes.com/job-searching-19-creative-ways-build-target-company-list/

HOW TO SEARCH FOR CONTACT INFORMATION AT TARGET FIRMS

1. Effective use of LinkedIn search tool

- Title: select titles of individuals who could be a prospective boss or involved in the hiring process
- Location: within target area zip codes
- Industry: choose target field(s)

2. Additional ways to find contact information

- Email address on profile page
- Use allotted InMail function selectively (if paid subscription)—determine if LinkedIn account is used often to evaluate if email will get read
- Referral function through network if confidentiality will not be breached
- Call company asking for contact directly
- Google the person's name to see if the email address is on another page
- Corporate website

- Look for another individual's email from target firm and mimic the format of other individuals (try PR, Sales, Accounts Receivable)
- Social media accounts / Blogs
- Search for conventions, meetings, or gatherings the person may have attended and see if they list contact information

3. Information at data websites—check each site for recent pricing, if applicable. Some recommendations, but these memberships are not required to work with Chameleon Resumes and are at your sole discretion to join, if you need access to more detailed information:

- Paid membership of LinkedIn gives you access to more info than the free membership
- Zoominfo.com
- DNB.com
- Corporate Alumni Groups (free)

Read this article:
Finding the Right Contacts for Your Job Search
www.chameleonresumes.com/finding-the-right-contacts-for-your-job-search-using-linkedin

USE LINKEDIN IN YOUR JOB SEARCH PLAN

Developing an Effective LinkedIn Presence

1. Create a contact list spreadsheet (or contact database, etc.) of all your contacts from all areas of your life—not just professional.

Consider these areas to pull contacts from:

- All past employers
- Fellow college, high school, and postgraduate alumni
- Previous college, high school, and postgraduate educators
- Community contacts from religious, civic, educational organizations
- Neighbors, friends, and family
- Vendors or services used from all past positions—paid and voluntary
- Past and current clients (minding any non-competes in place)
- Professional and service clubs and associations
- Volunteer engagement contacts

2. Join related **groups** to expand your reach:

- Targeted Industries (Real Estate, Mortgage, Banking, Insurance)
- Discipline Based (Sales, Business Development, Teaching, Training)
- Job Seeker / Job lead focused groups

3. Using your list of contacts, selectively increase your LinkedIn Connections list to at least 500 contacts using the list development tactics above.

4. Using content from your resume, develop your LinkedIn profile to communicate to your connections the type of role you're seeking. Bring your profile to 100%—or at least 90% at the minimum.

STEP 6: DESIGN & EXECUTE YOUR JOB LANDING PLAN

5. It is important to have a professional headshot for your profile. Do not use a cutout from a family photo or gala event. Have one done specifically for business purposes. It matters.

6. Get recommendations from as many of your connections as you can, paying particular attention to clients, superiors, subordinates, and corporate peers. These will tell prospective employers the type of employee you are.

7. Search your connections' contacts by using the "View Their Connections" button in the person's search result to view, search, and save your searches of their connections. This is a great way to find out if your key connections might introduce you to someone within your search parameters.

How to Create a LinkedIn Job Search and Turn it into a Daily Email Alert

1. Click on the Jobs tab on your profile.
2. Enter the title, skill, or company you are looking for.
3. Enter the location where you would like to work.
4. Click on SEARCH.
5. You will see a row of filters where you have the opportunity to set the parameters of your search.
6. Click All Filters to see all the parameters you can set.
7. Once you have set all your filters click Show Results.
8. At the top of the job search results, switch the Job alert toggle to On to create a job alert for your current search criteria.
9. Click the gear beside the Job alert toggle to edit the frequency of the alert via email and notifications.

LinkedIn People Search

LinkedIn gives you many criteria to identify prospects, but these criteria are not endless. The most valuable search tool LinkedIn gives you is the People Search Function.

Within the People Search, you can discover prospects via the following criteria:

- Keywords you come up with.
- Location including country and zip code. (Hint: Advance to the results page, you can filter for specific cities.)
- Titles.
- Company names.
- Schools attended.
- Industry.
- LinkedIn Groups They Belong To (as long as you are in the same group)
- Relationship (i.e. Degrees of Connection)
- Language
- Company Size
- Seniority Levels
- Interested In (things people say they're interested in, on their profile)
- Fortune level companies (if you're aiming at the big dogs)
- Open Link

If you don't understand how to use the system to search for people, you won't do well at mining the system for great prospects. Spend some time playing with the People Search and figure out what each criteria means.

STEP 6: DESIGN & EXECUTE YOUR JOB LANDING PLAN

HOW TO USE GOOGLE TO PERFORM EFFECTIVE JOB SEARCH RESEARCH JUST LIKE A RECRUITER

Track your target firms using Google with the following tools and tactics to find and follow the jobs, key people, and company information you'll need to stay ahead of your fellow job seekers.

When used properly, these tools can help you find recent job postings, latest company news, up-to-date contact information, and many other valuable pieces of data that can help you create strategy and execute your job search activities knowledgeably and effectively.

Here are some tactics used by recruiters and researchers:

Perform an X-Ray search: Google allows you to search a specific site on its own, rather than searching the entire web. This is an "X-Ray" search. In the Google search box, you can specify the site you want to search, using a format like:

site:www.linkedin.com

Then add whatever additional search terms you may want. For example, if you don't have many connections on LinkedIn, you might not get many results when you search within LinkedIn's own search tool. Perhaps you're looking for a company contact in your job search... like a marketing manager at Wrigley Corp. in the Chicago area. You could enter:

site:www.linkedin.com "Greater Chicago" "Marketing Manager" Wrigley

Among many directory pages and others, you'll also find the public LinkedIn profiles of anyone with "Marketing Manager" and "Wrigley" in their profile description, registered in the "Greater Chicago" area. You can also do an X-Ray search of specific companies you may be interested in pursuing, to find information on their sites that you are seeking.

Decode blind job ads—then apply to the company directly. You can take a blind job ad posted by a third party recruiter, without the employer's name, and cut and paste a phrase from the job ad into the Google Search field. If they posted the job on the company website, it will show up in search results directing you to the company posting the job.

Use Google Alerts: Google Alerts are an excellent way to be find new information about your target companies, as news breaks. If you're a senior accountant specializing in financial reporting and one of your target companies is PriceWaterhouseCoopers (PWC) in the Washington, DC area, you can simply set up an Alert for news searching "PriceWaterhouse", and anything posted anywhere with that string will trigger a notification to you.

For jobs, you can set up an Alert using an X-Ray search of their site's career pages. For example, if you're looking for a senior accountant position posted on the PWC website in the Scottsdale, Arizona area, you can set up an Alert string like: site:careers.pwc.com Scottsdale Arizona "Senior Accountant"

Most companies post positions on their own site before any external job boards, and often they don't post a position on external job boards at all. If you have notifications set up correctly, you'll see new positions before most everyone else!

You can set up as many Alerts as you'd like, for as many companies as you'd like, with as many variations of search words as you'd like... be creative, but do not overwhelm yourself! Too much information can cause some people to not take action until they have ALL the information—and we can never have ALL the information, so some never take action at all. Use caution and continually take action to reach your goals.

Consolidate your information with Feedly. This is an excellent way to keep track of company information, career blogs, and job postings.

Gmail is a great place to direct all your Google Alerts so you can read and follow up on them all from one central place, without filling up your email box and fielding constant interruptions.

Efficiently finding information from your target company sites, setting up automatic notifications, and reading all the relevant updates easily in one place makes Google an extremely powerful online resource to organize job search and develop your target list in a way most job seekers don't use.

USE SOCIAL MEDIA FOR THE MOST UP-TO-DATE INFORMATION AND REACH KEY DECISION MAKERS

- Follow companies that interest you and/or are on your target list.
- Research your target companies on social media. Social media is a great resource to help you prepare for your next interview.
- Follow people who work at those companies, especially those in the field where you want to work.
- Engage in conversation and offer knowledge to interact with those you follow and who follow you.

- Take part in related social media chats to create new relationships, receive insight, and get job leads. Establish yourself as a knowledge resource.

USING FACEBOOK IN YOUR JOB SEARCH

How to Use Facebook to Gain Information, Get Leads and Advance Your Job Search

<Like> the Facebook fan pages of companies where you'd like to work.

<Like> posts selectively and engage in smart, appropriate conversation via status updates when appropriate.

Complete your personal Facebook page and professional sections in a professional manner. Even though you may set your profile so others can't see it, if you're tagged on pictures, have others comment on your posts, or you comment on others' posts, you may be enabling others to see your profile. Use caution and ensure it is professional and appropriate.

Fill out your "About Me" section completely with your work history. This will help others network with you and see your employment history to evaluate.

By completing all the sections of a Facebook profile, you increase your chances of being found by recruiters.

HOW TO NETWORK EFFECTIVELY AND POWERFULLY

Leverage your background and interests to identify and determine which networking events to pursue and explore. Use eventbrite.com, meetup.com, and other association and alumni websites to find the right events for you. Once you've attended a few, select two or three groups at most to attend and network with regularly. It's through ongoing attendance, interaction, and follow-up that you form new contacts on a solid, genuine foundation that can lead to mutually beneficial lead and information exchange.

Some areas where you can look for networking event opportunities are:

- Corporate alumni
- Industry associations
- Professional discipline groups
- College alumni
- Community & location-based groups
- Hobby/sport based
- Non-profit volunteer based
- Professional development & training

Best Ways to Follow-Up after a Networking Event

So we know why we network, but what do you do to follow up after a networking event? After all, it's what you do after the event that matters, as that's where the proper work begins! Here are some suggestions:

1. Google their name—you'd be amazed at what you can find by Googling a person's name. You can find additional information to help you with reasons to connect—or not.
2. Make notes on what happened at the event and create a list of actions to implement.
3. Write an email to say you enjoyed meeting them and why it makes sense to keep chatting.

4. Reach out to stay in touch, if there's no need to meet—ask them what they thought of the event via email.
5. Connect with a LinkedIn invitation. Include a note saying you enjoyed meeting at the event.
6. Via email, suggest a 15-minute phone call. Be clear on the purpose and how it can benefit you both.
7. Here's a novel idea: just call the person... tell them you enjoyed meeting them and would like to keep the conversation going. Ask if they prefer a phone chat or coffee meeting as a follow-up.
8. Propose a face-to-face meeting over coffee right out of the gate with contacts that have the most potential, who interest you most, or simply where it makes sense. Show interest in them.
9. Follow the person on social media. This can provide real-time data to improve the content of your communication.
10. If you see a personal connection outside work and it makes sense, connect on Facebook.
11. Do not automatically add them to any email list you may have! Instead, email asking if they would like to join your email list since you thought, based on your conversation, the content may be of interest. Don't spam!
12. Enter the information into your contact management system. A contact made today may not bring you business today, but that person may be the resource you needed (or who needed you) for a situation in the future.
13. Look to influence. See how you can introduce two people who can help each other and ask to make that introduction... it's good karma, as you're always

remembered as the person who made the introduction.
14. Thank the host of the event—a great way to start a connection you did not have before.
15. Ideally make contact within 48 hours, but definitely reach out if it is later than that. I have reached out six months after an initial meeting and had it turn out well—but I don't recommend waiting that long!
16. Look for people who can influence your business or job search—not just hire you. Influencers are more impactful than direct clients or hiring managers, since they introduce many opportunities.
17. Search for collaborators. The best way to grow is by collaborating with others.
18. Send an article or book reference via email or snail mail. Show you were engaged in the conversation.

Networking can take time and energy if you let it, or you can integrate it into your daily activities more effortlessly with a simple change in mindset and habits. A small, consistent investment of time each week can pay off huge dividends in the future for you and your network. Take some actions above and see the good that happens.

ARE CAREER FAIRS & JOB EVENTS RIGHT FOR YOU?

Generally, I'm not a huge proponent of job fairs, unless it's for entry-level positions. Job fairs can be good resources when focused on the level and discipline that suit your needs. However, when you're conducting a confidential job search, consider not attending job fairs as resumes from participants are often distributed to all the companies taking part, which can jeopardize your confidentiality. Attend job or career fairs only if they're specifically tailored to your discipline, and the event advertises that it's seeking talent for positions at your level.

HOW TO EFFECTIVELY USE JOB BOARDS AND WEBSITES

Set up alerts on no more than four job boards and career websites, such as:

- www.indeed.com
- www.simplyhired.com
- www.ziprecruiter.com
- www.monster.com

And other profession-based or industry-based sites such as:

- www.mediabistro.com
- www.idealist.org
- www.efinancialcareers.com
- www.talentzoo.com (for marketing jobs)

When you set the alerts, you will receive jobs that match your search criteria when they are posted. This will save so much time, rather than trolling the boards manually looking for jobs. You shouldn't really spend more than one hour per week on job board postings.

Post your resume confidentially on one or two websites to increase your ability to be found by recruiters using these tools. Refrain from posting your resume everywhere or on over five websites, as this can dilute your brand for recruiters who use multiple tools and see you everywhere. It will also limit the number of calls from jobs you don't want if you're on a select number of sites.

GENERATING LEADS FROM ONLINE FORUMS/BLOGS/COMMUNITIES

Focus on finding and engaging audiences on career-related forums, blogs, and online communities unique to your industry and interests to expand your networking and contact base. General career advice blogs can be helpful, like www.chameleonresumes.com/blog for job search and career tips.

But to be even more effective for cultivating new contacts in your field and profession, search out industry contacts who write blogs then follow the conversations on these websites. When you have something thoughtful to contribute and/or have a question to ask, post thoughtful comments to the website to demonstrate your web-savvy and professional knowledge to your industry and discipline community. If you'd like to set up and write your own blog, let's chat about that—it's something I can help you with.

Read my article on how I got an interview simply by commenting on a blog post. It happens:

> www.chameleonresumes.com/how-i-landed-an-interview-without-even-trying

Listservs exist for almost every professional and are pervasive throughout local communities through Google Groups. They can be a very effective online networking tool. Recruiters post jobs, job seeker members post openings to help fellow members, questions are posted for a community answer, and industry knowledge is shared. These are amazing forums to take part in and generate leads from through active contribution.

HOW TO BEST USE THIRD-PARTY RECRUITERS AND SEARCH FIRMS

When you're working, a third-party recruiter can be helpful if you're pursuing the same job or a promotion in the same field. When you're looking to change careers or currently are not working, a third-party recruiter will not be helpful for direct hire work, but possibly for contract work.

Recruiters will seek you out on LinkedIn if you fit the profile their client wants. A third-party recruiter will not "find you a job." Third-party recruiters work for the hiring company, as that is who pays them, not the candidate. So this strategy should only be a small part of your overall job search plan. Continue with the actions suggested in this book first to create and manifest your own leads and manage your target company list.

For contract work, the following agencies can be an excellent source for contacting about temporary or consulting work:

- www.randstad.com
- www.kellyservices.com
- www.roberthalf.com
- www.manpower.com
- www.kforce.com
- www.hiredynamics.com
- www.rothstaffing.com
- www.teksystems.com
- www.us.hudson.com

When your job search lands you an interview, you want to be

STEP 6: DESIGN & EXECUTE YOUR JOB LANDING PLAN

as well prepared as possible—so let's move onto the final step: mastering the interview mindset.

STEP 7: MASTER THE INTERVIEW MINDSET TO LAND THE JOB
BELIEVE YOU CAN LAND A JOB ON YOUR TERMS

Landing a job on your terms is not out of your reach. Simply put: if you believe you can do it, you can do it! This is the essential starting point for your job search.

You may not yet know how you'll get there or what specific steps to take but you must believe that, with the help of this book and other resources, you can land a job that will complement your needs, desires, and life choices. Without this basic belief, landing a job on your terms will be very difficult to accomplish. However, if you will believe you can do it and the powers of the universe will work with you in your quest, then you've successfully accomplished the crucial first step in landing a job on your terms.

Of course, you already have this belief to some degree, or you would not have invested in this book. So congratulations! You're already making progress toward your goal!

STEP 7: MASTER THE INTERVIEW MINDSET TO LAND THE JOB

DEFINE YOUR TERMS

The next step to landing a job on your terms is to know what your terms are. It's crucial to understand what you value in a job and it's just as important to have a clear perspective on what you do *not* want in a job. Many people start a job search without really knowing what they do and don't want. Without knowing their terms, job seekers accept positions only to discover they're unhappy with the duties, compensation packages, or corporate culture that accompany the new position.

Both parts of the equation—defining what you want and what you don't want—are equally essential to landing a job on your terms and avoiding emotional and professional turmoil.

Define What You Want

Make a list of what you want from your next position. What you desire will usually emerge if you look at a few areas that directly affect your life.

Some ideas to consider are:

- **Financial requirements:** You may want to make a certain amount of money. You know this compensation is within the realm of the skill set, abilities, and experience you possess. Maybe you've not received a raise in three years and you realize you won't receive one at your current employer for reasons beyond your control. You might then put on your list that you want a 10% raise because you've done research that shows you have the skills and expertise to warrant this compensation bump.

- **Career path:** You may need to develop certain skills and connections in order to attain your long-term professional goals. Let's say that currently you're an oncology drug sales representative and your long-term goal is to manage a sales team within a firm that sells oncology drugs. You might then decide to seek sales management jobs for products that support other diseases in order to gain management experience, then come back to oncology once you have this expertise. Sales management opportunities would then be an important item to add to your list.
- **Lifestyle needs:** You may need to land a role that supports your personal life. For example, you may need to work nights, or be home by 3 pm, or work from home 2-3 days per week. You may want a job that provides a company car you can also use for personal trips. It may be important to find a company that offers health insurance or tuition reimbursement. These points would go on your list.
- **Work style preferences:** Do you like to work in team environments? Do you prefer to work on your own? Do you like companies that value in-person meetings at the office or do you not want to travel to an office? Think long and hard about the situations that have suited you in the past and those where you were frustrated—and determine which options should be on your list.
- **Corporate culture:** Do you want an employer that values those who put their jobs first? Or do you want a role at a company where everyone who works there values a work/life balance? Do you want a job that will push you to

make strides quickly in your career? Or do you want a job that will take second place to your full personal life? I have been in both situations and I can see the pros and cons of each, but it's important that you know what matters to you.

Here are a few additional requirements you may have:

- **Flextime scheduling:** It may not matter to you how many hours you work over 40 hours, but perhaps you need flexibility in coming and going to accommodate your family life.
- **Minimum salary:** You may decide you need a salary above a certain amount for any new job to be worth making the move. Make sure, however, that your desired salary is based on market realities. Do the research to determine whether your skills, abilities, and experiences warrant the salary you desire; otherwise, you may waste your time.
- **Company size:** Your long-term goal may be to work in a major, world-class corporation. If you are currently at a Fortune 1000 company, you may need to move to a much larger company in order to gain the cultural experience that will allow you to end up at a Fortune 500 company. Company size would then be an important point to add to your list.

Define What You Don't Want

You may think, "Why should I outline what I don't want? It's simply the opposite of what I want." Well, for some people, this may be true. I've found, however, that for most people, what they want and what they do not want are two entirely different lists. Here are some examples of how the two lists can diverge:

- You may not want to travel overnight for your job—but day trips outside the office are ok with you. So overnight travel will be on your "don't want" list, but day trips, while ok with you, would probably never make your "want" list.
- You may not want to work in a cubicle, but you don't care if you have your own office, work in a group table setting, or work remotely at home—as long as you're not stuck in a tiny cube!
- You may not want to work past 6 pm at night, but it's fine if the company wants you in occasionally at 7 am. I am sure, however, that getting in at 7 am regularly would not be on your "want" list.

Why Are These Lists Important?

The lists of what you want and don't want will define your job search parameters, interview answers, and compensation package negotiations. Without these spelled out, you have no way:

- To define yourself to a prospective employer—this allows the employer to determine if you are a good fit for their company.
- To leverage and negotiate a fair package for the role for which you are being considered.
- To make yourself a memorable candidate for a prospective employer. The more one-size-fits-all you appear, the less appealing you are to an employer. You must be distinctive to be memorable.

STEP 7: MASTER THE INTERVIEW MINDSET TO LAND THE JOB

- To avoid taking a job that does not meet your financial, professional, personal, and lifestyle needs.

Your lists will help you evaluate job opportunities and plan answers for interviews. Without these parameters, it may be tempting to consider jobs that do not fit your needs. You may then find yourself in a position that makes you unhappy in the months and years to come.

REJECTION – WHAT IT IS AND WHAT IT ISN'T

The bottom line is: do not turn all rejections you experience into a negative reflection of who you are and your skills and experience. Frankly, it often is not that and all you're doing is negatively affecting your mindset. Review your list of needs and wants and don't wants to help you handle rejection and maintain a positive mindset while looking for a job on your terms.

Often, a job offer doesn't come because the candidate was not the right fit because the needs and wants of the company didn't match the needs and wants of the candidate.

Clients, friends and associates who are job-searching will frequently say to me, "Ugh, I didn't get that job I applied for." I ask them the following questions to help them stay rooted in facts and stay positive:

Do you know for a fact that someone else has filled the job?

Do you see on LinkedIn the name of someone newly hired, with the title of the job you sought? That would be proof. Did an announcement or press release go out naming the new hire in the role for which you interviewed? That would also be proof.

Without proof, they haven't filled the job yet. If that's the case, you haven't been rejected... yet.

Are you sure the job is closed?

Find out if the job is still open. Especially in a challenging economy, companies may freeze their hiring budget. If the job is closed and they didn't hire anyone, then no-one was rejected for the role.

Are they still interviewing for the job?

Has the company ceased interviewing without making a hire? They may have put the position on hold. If they're not considering anyone for the role at this point and no decision is going to be made, no-one has been rejected.

When you interviewed, did you find you didn't want the job?

If you discovered you wouldn't want the job, and they then didn't offer you the job, were you really rejected? Does it matter that they didn't select you for a job you wouldn't have wanted?

When you interviewed, did you feel concerns about the position or the company?

Were you put off by anything the interviewer said? Did the company or job seem too unstructured or structured for you? Did the employer cite concerns about your educational or professional credentials? Were they seeking someone with a specific degree you don't possess? Did the employer say they wanted someone with expertise handling specific situations that you haven't

STEP 7: MASTER THE INTERVIEW MINDSET TO LAND THE JOB

encountered before? If you had concerns about the job or the company, or if you felt the employer had concerns about your candidacy, you just may not be a good fit for that role. If you weren't a good fit, were you really rejected?

SO WHAT IS REJECTION?

After considering what rejection is not, I should tell you what I think rejection is, right? With job searching, rejection is:

If you wanted the job, were perfectly qualified according to the firm's requirements, and still did not get the job, then you were rejected.

While it is painful, there is nothing wrong with rejection. Getting rejected is part of life's natural selection process and is an inevitable by-product of making any sort of effort. You will be rejected from jobs. But why carry more rejection baggage than you need to?

If you didn't want the job, you were not rejected. If the job is still open, you were technically not rejected. If you had concerns about your background, education, or qualifications not measuring up to what they wanted, then you may not have fit the job's parameters. Avoiding a poor fit is sometimes labeled as rejection, and this can affect your ability to continue the job search with a positive spirit.

I suggest you view the job search as a quest for the right fit, rather than as a test of whether you are acceptable. This is where your list of needs/wants and don't wants can be especially helpful.

Example:

With the list of your needs/wants and don't wants, you can redefine what "getting rejected for a job" really means. Let's look at how this helps you.

Here are the sample lists of a job seeker named Jonathan. These are his wants:

- Wants to land a job as a marketing manager for a start-up firm focused on healthcare drug development that capitalizes on his oncology background.
- Needs to work remotely from home.
- Wants to work with an international team, specifically Asia and/or Europe.
- Needs a minimum salary of $95,000 plus incentives.

And his don't wants:

- Does not want to travel more than 15% of the year.
- Does not want to work in pediatric disease drug development.
- Does not want to use a corporate issued smart phone—wants to use his own.

Now we have a list of wants and don't wants, let's assume Jonathan lands interviews with four start-up drug firms over the course of two weeks. He does not advance in any of the roles. Here are the reasons he didn't land the job, for each company:

1. Syntegic Therapeutics: Requires travel 2 weeks per month.
2. Compass Technologies: Wants expertise in immunology, which he doesn't have.
3. Etanics, Inc.: Has a conservative, big-brother type technology policy.
4. Dyson Biotechnology Advisors: Base salary caps out at $135,000.

STEP 7: MASTER THE INTERVIEW MINDSET TO LAND THE JOB

When you compare Jonathan's lists to the reasons he did not advance in the interview process at these companies, do you think he was rejected? I don't think so. He was simply not the right fit for the company and/or the company was not the right fit for him.

This exercise can help you develop and maintain a positive mindset as you look for the right job. Unnecessarily labeling your experiences as "rejection" can take its toll when you're applying to multiple positions and preparing for interviews. Do not apply the rejection label lightly. Use it only when it's applicable. And when it truly applies, use the experience to learn how you can improve your candidacy and perform better next time around.

PREPARING FOR INTERVIEWS TO SET YOURSELF APART FROM THE COMPETITION

The purpose of a company interview is twofold:

1. To learn whether you are a good cultural and performance fit for the company.
2. To see your response when handling stress—because an interview is a stressful situation.

An interview showcases your knowledge and your ability to think quickly. The company is also evaluating how you present yourself in important situations. The interviewer assumes that the way you conduct yourself in the interview will be the way you conduct yourself with company executives, staff, vendors, and clients. So if you do something that seems questionable in the interview, they will assume you're at risk of doing something similar with other people.

An interview can help you find out if this is a company you would like to join. Through discussion and questions, you can determine if this opportunity is a match for your skill set, professional goals, and lifestyle choices. Do not think the company holds all the cards. However, to ensure you get the chance to choose, you must play the interview game through to the end, which means you must start by thoroughly preparing for the meeting.

In today's economic climate, simply Googling the company before an interview will not set you apart from other candidates, and checking out the company's webpage no longer cuts it. In fact, a savvy interviewer can now tell if that's all you did. This type of minimal effort will reflect poorly on your candidacy and put you towards the bottom of the list.

Defining your needs/wants and don't wants in the manner discussed earlier and preparing for the interview as outlined below will best position you to move successfully through the interview process. You will then be equipped to make accurate decisions and secure a job on your terms.

How much time do you need to prepare?

I am often asked how much time to allocate to interview preparation. There is no precise, formulaic answer. I wish I could say, "Prepare for X amount of time and you will definitely land the role." But there are some suggested time-frames to consider:

- Set aside a minimum of 3-5 hours to research the company, the position for which you are interviewing, and the interviewer(s).
- Allocate 5-10 hours to researching yourself and your preferences, and to practicing your answers to a full range of interview questions. This will prepare you to think effectively on your feet in an interview.

STEP 7: MASTER THE INTERVIEW MINDSET TO LAND THE JOB

It is at this point I might see raised eyebrows. You probably understand and accept the need to research the company, the position, and the interviewer. But when I suggest spending 5-10 hours educating yourself on, well, yourself, this is when I get the perplexed looks.

"I already know my background and myself, so why do I need to study myself?" may be the question in your mind. But the secret to successfully landing a job on your terms lies in the work you devote to answering this question.

Why you need to study yourself

I performed an informal poll of 50 clients and students, asking them the following questions regarding a recent interview they had:

1. What percentage of time did you spend discussing your background? Most answered 75% or more.
2. What percentage of time did you spend discussing the company's products, history, or performance? Most answered less than 30% of the time.

Note: This was not a scientific poll, nor were these numbers supposed to add up to 100% even if it was a precise survey.

Candidates generally approach an interview thinking they need to prove to the prospective employer that they have exhaustively researched the firm and know everything there is to know about it. Yet most interviewers and hiring managers will not spend much time asking candidates to demonstrate this knowledge.

Hiring managers and interviewers already know their company. Yes, they may want to test how interested you are in the company and they may want to see whether you can apply your expertise to their organization. But generally, most interviewers will ask questions about you, your background, your preferences, your experiences, your achievements, your challenges, your failures, and how you can bring value to their corporation. Therefore:

Spend most of your prep time reviewing your background and practicing answers that show how you can make a positive difference to the company if hired.

Researching you

We prepare in this way in order to minimize the risk of having to think about something for the very first time during the interview. The goal is to have thought of most possible questions and practiced the best possible answers *before* the interview. You cannot predict every question, of course, but if you're prepared with clear and confident answers, you will think more effectively on your feet and your self-assurance will radiate though the interview.

Know your resume backwards, forwards and every angle in between:

- **Be intimately familiar with every bullet in your resume.** For each bullet in your resume, write out the story or a few examples outlining how you performed or achieved that bullet. Be able to succinctly and articulately communicate the story behind each bullet.
- **Readily know the numbers associated with each bullet** and the information behind the numbers. To leave the most favorable impression with your interviewer, take the numbers listed one step further

STEP 7: MASTER THE INTERVIEW MINDSET TO LAND THE JOB

and know how they came about. For example, if you know you increased sales by 23%, know what the starting and ending revenue numbers were, which markets contributed to the increase and what changes you made to get the increase.
- **Prepare stories about challenges, failures, and difficult situations that are not on your resume.** These types of questions always come up. Embrace this and be ready for those questions. We will address specifics related to these in the "Face the Most Difficult Questions Fearlessly" section.

Prepare answers to the standard interview questions and be able to instantly recall these answers:

Tell me about yourself.

This is by far the most mundane question, and it often reveals that your interviewer is inexperienced or unimaginative. Nonetheless, you must be ready for this question with a concise, all-inclusive answer. Please do not start with your early years—the hiring manager is not asking for your biography.

However, this is an opportunity to validate why they decided to see you. Offer a brief professional synopsis of your professional history and proudest achievements, along with a quick anecdote that adds something appropriately personal.

Why did you leave your last job?

If the reason you left is neutral or positive, express it confidently without revealing personal information—keep it professionally focused.

If the reason is negative, be prepared to present it in a neutral, but truthful, light. The prospective employer does not need to know all the sordid details.

A brief, diplomatic, and neutral answer is the best way to move the conversation along, so the hiring manager does not feel the need to delve further.

When preparing to answer why you left your last job, consider whether your explanation could set off alarm bells for the interviewer. Could this same reason interfere with your new job?

For example, if you left your last job to stay home with your family or to care for a sick relative, you risk having the employer think you might leave again if you add to your family or your relative needs care again.

While it is illegal for an employer to factor this information into a hiring decision, interviewers are human. They can make poor decisions, consciously or unconsciously, given the opportunity. I suggest keeping the reason neutral, such as, "I left my last position to be available full time for a family situation that required my attention. However, that situation has been definitively rectified, which is why I am looking to return to work full time."

Why do you want to leave your current job?

If you are currently working, be sure your reasons for wanting to leave are rooted in advancing your career and professional development.

You should clearly explain how the prospective company will benefit from you pursuing these goals. The reasons should not be based on personality conflicts, comfort or convenience issues, compensation or benefits.

STEP 7: MASTER THE INTERVIEW MINDSET TO LAND THE JOB

Describe your ideal boss or work arrangement.

Be sure to describe a manager profile or a work arrangement that exists at the company—especially if the company is one where you want to work. On the other hand, do not simply say what they want to hear—or you may get hired and realize you don't enjoy working for their type of boss or work culture.

However, if you want the job and you are flexible, be sure to describe a person or place that exists within that organization. Set the company up to succeed in making you happy if they hire you.

Why are you pursuing a role you've done before?

In explaining why you are pursuing a role you have done before, don't put your prospective manager's job down when describing why you're not pursuing the higher level job. If they ask why you do not want to manage any longer, be sure that you don't denigrate the job your prospective manager has—or inadvertently appear to be looking down on your potential manager. No-one really wants to hire someone who has that been-there-done-that feel and makes the manager feel dumb or inadequate.

Be sure to answer from a point of wanting to contribute at a different level and talk about how you want to make someone else look good as you know how it feels to be supported by a great team in your previous roles.

What are your strengths?

What personality traits have contributed to your success? This is an opportunity to sell yourself and provide concrete, specific examples of work experiences that demonstrate your strengths. Stick to strengths that complement the position for which you're applying. Ensure they're relevant to the organization, the job and the company's goals.

What areas do you need to further develop or need training in?

This is the "What are your weaknesses?" question in a positive guise. Answer the question in a similar, positive but sincere manner: "I would benefit from public speaking training" or "I could benefit from time management classes so I don't take on too many projects."

Answer this question as you would any question about your deficiencies:

1. Remember that everyone has weaknesses, so don't refuse to acknowledge yours.
2. Do not bring up a weakness that could suggest you would not perform well at the job.
3. Demonstrate how you have improved your skill set or compensated for your weakness to ensure it is never an issue at the job.

What do you like to do outside of work?

Be genuine in this answer. It is a chance for the hiring manager to see you as a person and not as just another applicant. The smart way to approach this question is to choose a hobby that can define you as interesting, driven, self-motivated, or unique. It should add dimension to you as a person. Do not bring up any activity that is controversial, based on politics or religion, displays poor judgment, depicts you as lazy, or could interfere with your job performance or attendance.

STEP 7: MASTER THE INTERVIEW MINDSET TO LAND THE JOB

Tell me about a typical day/week/month in your job at X company.

What did you like most/least about your last role? Be colorful and specific when describing what you do in a day/week/month at your job. Assume the interviewer has no idea what you do. Even if they know what a marketing manager does at their company, they have no idea what that entails at your company. So do not assume they know—they don't.

Offering a descriptive picture of your work activities, interactions and results shows the hiring manager that you have a great understanding of your role and take pride in your position. People who provide vague or general answers either did not do the job as stated, are not proud of what they did, or are poor communicators of what they did—none of which is attractive to an employer.

As a side note, the worst possible answer, in my opinion, is, "I did everything." Never say that. It tells the hiring manager nothing more than that you are full of yourself. Offer specifics if you want to make a positive impact.

Tell me about a problem you had with a client/boss/employee and how you handled it.

Companies want to hire inventive, resilient employees who can troubleshoot unexpected situations effectively with little or no drama in the workplace. Employers do not expect prospective employees to have never had a problem—everyone runs into difficulties at work. But you set yourself apart from other applicants when you demonstrate your skill in handling these problems and your ability to learn from them.

Describe a time you and your boss disagreed on a project and how you handled yourself. Outline a customer complaint that arose, how you identified the problem, and how you fixed it. Diplomatically describe working with a confrontational employee and how you resolved the situation or even turned it around. Describe your experience in a neutral, humble, and solution-driven manner.

Your answers and demeanor will tell the interviewer how you will perform when problems arise in their company.

Why do you want to work for us?

To effectively answer this question, you have research yourself and the interviewing company thoroughly. Once you have this research under your belt, you can provide an answer that demonstrates how your experience and abilities make an excellent match for the company and the position it is seeking to fill. Show the compatibility between your aspirations and the company's objectives.

Simply put, if you hit your goals, the company will hit their goals. Companies want to hire employees whose personal goals align with the goals of the organization.

Why should we hire you?

This is your time to shine. Based on the research you've done and the information you've gleaned from the interview, outline succinctly how your experience and skills will allow you to fully satisfy the company's needs. Describe how you will bring value by helping them exceed their goals.

The answer you give should put to rest in the interviewer's mind, "Is this the right candidate? The best candidate? How do I know?"

STEP 7: MASTER THE INTERVIEW MINDSET TO LAND THE JOB

If you answer those questions for the interviewer, you will advance to the next level, or if this is the final interview, they will offer you the job.

When answering questions posed by the interviewer, don't pontificate about how you used to do things. Do not reference past incidents in a reminiscing or nostalgic capacity. When answering an interview question, describe a past experience objectively and diplomatically. Do not reminisce or pontificate. no-one wants to hire a blowhard or a know-it-all.

Always be curious about new approaches or situations and do not make it seem like all your previous solutions will solve all future problems. You will come across like you could be blindsided by thinking you know and have done everything.

Ask about what issues are motivating the company to make the hire. Then outline how you can solve the current issues. Inquire about what challenges the company is currently experiencing and ask diagnostic questions humbly and inquisitively, where appropriate. You want to show how you would approach a problem without making the employer feel stupid that they didn't think of what you might ask... you want your questions to come across like you're trying to be helpful.

RESEARCHING THE COMPANY

Researching the company is a must, and almost all job candidates do it today. However, many candidates do not do the work thoroughly or methodically—which presents an opportunity for the motivated job seeker. I will address here some of the basic steps to ensure your efforts are thorough, but I also provide many less obvious research tools to ensure you stand out from other applicants.

The emphasis in all my tips is that you shouldn't simply study the information outlined in corporate, public, and third-party sources. Anyone can do that. The interview is not a test to see whether you read the company website. Instead, you want to identify opportunities and show how you can add value to the company if they hire you.

Take the information you gain through your research and prepare insightful questions and observations that can serve as discussion points during the interview. Here are some ways to do that:

Check the company website for information—and not just in the usual places.

Don't just check out the company history and mission statement—look at every page on the website and try to deduce where the company is headed and how you can contribute to their mission.

Review the company's products and services and get a handle on how they present themselves to the marketplace. What image do they put forth?

Get a sense of the management's career histories and see what professional and educational credentials the firm values. Are executives home grown and have been with the company for a while? Do they get recruited from competitors? Are their backgrounds a little unorthodox for the position they hold?

Look at all the job openings. What kinds of positions are being filled? Does this tell you anything about the company or give you information about its direction? For example, you may notice the company seems to be expanding its sales force. If you're

STEP 7: MASTER THE INTERVIEW MINDSET TO LAND THE JOB

interviewing for a training role, you could then indicate you have observed that many salespeople may be hired and ask how the company expects the training team to contribute to their onboarding.

Google the company's name for articles written by third parties.

Look for third-party commentary and see how it supplements, supports or contradicts the information written by the company. This outside information can offer additional insights. How is the third-party information different or similar to the company's take on the same subjects?

Research stories about the company on Forbes.com, Fortune.com, huffingtonpost.com, major news outlets, and industry publications. Do they contain comments made by the company's spokespeople? This will give you a sense of the interviewer's opinions on these stories.

The Better Business Bureau can be a helpful source of information for smaller companies with whom you may be interviewing.

Google the company's name and the words <complaints>, <problems>, <unhappy employees>, or <scam> if you have any concerns about the company. This will reveal whether any adverse information has been documented or written about the firm.

Look up the firm on glassdoor.com to find out what its employees say.

Examine the stats provided by these sites and read what employees say about the firm. If you find negative points, are these things you can live with—or better yet, would you thrive within that type of environment? One person's "boring job" may be another person's "stable employer."

Remember to take the information in its context, as every firm has unhappy employees and these may be the ones who take the time to write negative commentary.

Review financial information if the company is public, on edgar-online.com or Yahoo Finance.

This is a crucial action, regardless of the position to which you are applying. It is imperative to understand the business and financial underpinnings of any potential employer.

If you are a creative professional, do not think you're excused from understanding the financials of a company. You should understand how your creative contributions affect the company's top and bottom lines. Knowing the business of your craft is one of the best ways you can differentiate yourself as a creative professional.

If you are a financial or business professional, take time to review the company's overall financial position. Showing you have some understanding even of areas that you won't be directly responsible for, is a key way to differentiate yourself as a solid business person.

Follow the company prior to the interview on Instagram, Facebook, LinkedIn, and other relevant social media.

What is the company talking about? What is it posting? Are there any obvious and underlying themes? Can you apply any of your previous experiences to some of these topics being discussed on social media channels?

Are they featuring promotions, sales, special events or product launches? How could you contribute to their success?

Are they particularly proud of a charitable initiative in which they are involved? What can you offer this initiative? Be prepared to discuss it.

Consider speaking to past or current employees of the company, and to people from the department to which you are applying.

Be selective here. Use your judgment and consider the source of the information when you do this.

You can use LinkedIn to find past and current employees and discover how you are connected to them. You can then evaluate if an introduction would be helpful and prudent.

Have a strong handle on the firm's position in its marketplace and how it ranks compared to its competitors.

It is not enough to simply know who the company's competitors are. Take it further by understanding how the marketplace views the company and how its customers rate it.

If this information is not available publicly, do your own research. Speak to contacts in the industry, gather their impressions and observations, and ask for suggestions.

RESEARCHING THE INTERVIEWER

When interviewing, one of your goals is to create rapport with the interviewer and begin cultivating a relationship. Researching the interviewer can give you insights to use during your conversation. Keep in mind that some of this information may not be usable. But having the information is better than not having it: the insights can help you say the right thing and avoid committing a gaffe.

Research the person on LinkedIn and Google.

Look for conversation points and common interests. File these in the back of your mind to use if the opportunity presents itself.

See if they have attended any professional conferences recently, as that could make for an interesting discussion about industry trends and best practices.

Explore whether you have worked for the same or competitor organizations.

Determine if you share the same alma mater. In most cases, this piece of information can be a good thing to reference. However, not everyone had a positive experience in college, as I was reminded when one of my clients mentioned to an interviewer that they'd gone to the same school. Apparently, the interviewer did not share her enthusiasm for the school, and this cast a dark cloud over the rest of the interview.

Become familiar with the person's career path.

This can be good information for interviews with the management and people you may work with, if hired.

You can determine whether to ask them how they achieved their success or ask for their experiences with certain initiatives.

Use information from Facebook and other personal websites with caution.

If you find your interviewer has a public Facebook account and has (knowingly or unknowingly) told the world that she breeds

STEP 7: MASTER THE INTERVIEW MINDSET TO LAND THE JOB

Great Danes or that he recently took his four children to Vermont, think twice before bringing up this information. You may wish to demonstrate your superb research skills, but the interviewer may come away thinking you are a creepy stalker who is trying to bond superficially.

Dropping information found from social media channels can be the equivalent of name-dropping to prove what and who you know. It can make you look immature and unsophisticated and may not advance your candidacy forward.

If the interviewer mentions they recently went to Vermont, by all means ask about the trip. Or if asked about your hobbies, you may bring up your passion for competing in the Westminster Dog Show with your prize chocolate labrador. But use judgment when showing what you have discovered about the person who is interviewing you.

RESEARCHING THE POSITION

Thoroughly understanding the position for which you are applying is essential. With this information, you can outline point by point how your experiences and credentials will enable you to successfully perform the role. How do you learn all you can about the open role?

Ask the corporate human resources contact or the search firm recruiter for the job description.

You want to do this for two reasons:

1. The job description is different from the job ad posting. The job ad posting is written to attract candidates to apply to the company. The job description defines the expectations, credentials, and requirements needed to be successful in the role.

2. As a former recruiter, I was always more impressed with candidates who asked for a job description, versus those who did not ask. It showed me who was going the extra mile. Knowing the job description allows you to explain how you can perform each aspect of the role, with examples drawn from your experience. So give yourself the advantage and ask for it. If the corporate HR contact or the search firm recruiter does not have it or cannot provide it, don't fret. It is still better to ask than not to ask.

Research the job title at competitor firms.

Job titles may mean different things at different companies. A director of marketing in one company may oversee some aspect of sales, whereas in another firm, the director of marketing reports into the sales department, and in yet a third company, the director of marketing may be a peer to the director of sales.

Get a sense of the job's responsibilities and how other firms structure this role. You will not bring up the other firms during your interview, but the information can shed light on how the position is structured and can help you make sure that you want this job.

Prepare examples of how you have performed or would perform each aspect listed on the job description.

Be ready to provide tactical examples of how you can successfully perform the duties and requirements listed.

Write these points down as preparation for the interview. I suggest writing on paper, rather than just thinking about them. This will help organize your thoughts. The first time you come up with your examples should NOT be during the actual interview. Write out and practice saying these points.

Use LinkedIn to find people who used to hold the position title for which you are interviewing.

You are not looking to connect with these people and this will probably not be information you will share in the interview, but look at that person's background. What were their past positions? What is this person's education? Do you have a similar or different background?

Do you have the impression that the new person being hired will be expected to fix a problem, grow a unit, or create something new? Does it seem to you that the person who previously held the position could not do this—or did it well?

Is it a good thing your background is similar (the company wants someone with a similar experience set) or a bad thing (the company wants someone from a different industry or business angle)? In either case, you must demonstrate that your experience is appropriate and valuable.

WHAT TO WEAR TO IMPRESS ON YOUR INTERVIEW

I know that job seekers reading this book are pretty savvy, and you might think that we don't need to cover this topic, given all the information available on the subject. But with all the changes in corporate dress standards, the divergence of company cultures, and the rise of freelancing, it turns out that interview attire is something that can never be covered enough.

Here's the basic rule: what you are wearing during your job interview should never distract from your purpose, which is to convey that you are the right candidate for the open role. Standing out on an interview is important—but you do not want your clothes to do that for you. The key point to keep in mind:

Your clothes should not be louder than you.

If you wear the right outfit to an interview, people will most likely not notice what you wore. But if you wear the wrong thing to an interview, your outfit could be the only thing the interviewer remembers—which would be a disaster. If the discussion following your interview is about what you wore, as opposed to what you can do, you have missed your opportunity.

When deciding what to wear to an interview, remember that you always want to be the most formally dressed person in the room. This is true regardless of whether you're going into a conservative environment or a casual one. I am not referring to ballroom formal here—I'm talking about effort. Put another way: the interviewer should not look more pulled together than the job seeker. For instance, the interviewer should not be wearing khakis and a blue button-down shirt, while the interviewee is wearing jeans and a blue button-down shirt. The other way around, however, is acceptable.

Here are some tips to help you steer the right course:

For traditional companies and corporate positions

- A blue or black suit is still very much the standard for both men and women. Pants suits for women are acceptable.
- Keep complementary items (shirts, blouses, ties) to neutrals such as white, cream, oxford blue, or navy blue.

- Shoes should be conservative and match the suit in most cases. For women, shoes should be heeled and closed-toed.
- Jewelry and accessories: Watches should be professional looking, with a leather or metal band; no plastic bands. Earrings, bracelets, and necklaces should be close to the body and conservative. Do not wear anything dangling or noisy.
- Perfume or cologne: I say avoid it. The interviewer may dislike your choice, or worse, have an allergy or sensitivity to the scent you are wearing.

For creative companies and positions

When interviewing at a creative company or for a creative position (i.e. art director, head designer, designer, graphic artist), it can be challenging to demonstrate your design flair without bringing negative attention to yourself. You probably need to be stylish in your attire and presentation materials, but you risk making the wrong choices. If you're going for this type of interview, however, you have probably accepted this risk. You may not land the job if you don't take the risk of standing out.

Here are ways to optimize your chances of taking the right sartorial risk:

- Do your research and use your judgment. If you're interviewing at a progressive technology start-up and your recruiter says, "Don't wear a suit," then do not wear a suit. Khakis and a crisp, blue button-down shirt are acceptable.
- Even if your research reveals that everyone wears jeans and T-shirts to work, I would still not wear jeans and a

T-shirt to the interview. Unless you are specifically told by a reputable employee contact, recruiter, or HR to wear jeans and a T-shirt, you should still err on the side of conservative and wear khakis and a crisp, button-down shirt.
- If you are interviewing for a creative role in a fashion or accessories company, wearing items that demonstrate your creativity or use of their product line is smart. Abide by the rule that "your clothes should not be louder than you" and you will be just fine.
- For women, wearing skirts or dresses in interviews with more casual companies is acceptable, as long as the outfit is tastefully accessorized and confidently pulled together.

Accessories for any interview

An interview is where you are supposed to put forth your best efforts. If your best includes questionable choices, the employer is left wondering what will happen once they hire you. Remember, the choices you make for an interview reflect the quality of your judgment.

Here are general tips to keep in mind when preparing for your interview:

- Bring a leather (or similar looking material) portfolio with a pad of paper, pen, and section to keep business cards (your own and those you receive).
- Have 5 to 10 copies of your resume and a list of references with company, title, relationship, and contact information.

- Carry one bag—this holds true even for women. Carrying more than one bag can look sloppy. The exception to this is if the candidate needs to carry a portfolio or laptop for the interview. But in these cases, make sure that all items look professional and presentable.
- Make sure everything fits properly: no ill-fitting clothing or accessories.
- Double-check clothing and accessories by sitting, standing, and walking around to ensure your outfit is comfortable and modest in all situations. You do not want to be tugging at your waistband, neckline, skirt hem, or shirt buttons. Give your outfit a test drive before the event.
- Have clothes cleaned and pressed professionally before each interview.
- Smile! Always go into the interview with a great outlook, a positive mindset, and a smile on your face. Employers want to hire people with good energy who will contribute positively to the company.
- Do not over-answer any question. Offer your answer conversationally, but do not provide too much information: this suggests insecurity, nervousness, or a desire to please. Confidence comes from knowing when you said enough, and then stopping.

FACE THE DIFFICULT QUESTIONS FEARLESSLY

Over the past few years, many people have had to face job and income losses, lowered expectations and results, client losses, workforce reductions, offices closing, and more. If you have experienced these difficulties, you are in good company.

Employed individuals going into job interviews today often have concerns about how to handle questions regarding disappointing personal or company track records over the past three or four years.

Unemployed candidates must enter interviews carrying the psychological baggage that comes from being without a job. They wonder how to respond when asked why they haven't been hired, why they were released in the first place, whether they have maintained their skills, etc.

So the best way to approach a job search under these conditions is to remember:

Relatively few people can claim a linear, progressive, and positive career path over the past few years. In fact, I believe most people have experienced some minor to significant professional setbacks.

You will reduce your anxieties about job interviews if you accept these two ideas:

1. People hire people they like. Be personable and likable, so the hiring manager feels like they can work with you each day. If the hiring manager likes you, it can overcome many perceived issues with a candidate's background. You will be surprised what a hiring manager will put aside if they connect well with the candidate and feel they can work with the person every day. Do not underestimate this.
2. Accept any setbacks you've experienced because of the economic downturn and be prepared to discuss them gracefully, honestly, and diplomatically. After all, you cannot avoid talking about your recent work history; if

you do, hiring managers will think you're hiding something. And all other things being equal, I believe the candidate who can speak positively about their challenges wins the game. Your honesty and self-confidence will increase your creditability with the hiring manager. It will also show how you would conduct yourself as an employee if hired.

If your recent past contains setbacks, do not hide them and simply hope the interviewer will not ask about them. It is far better to fully expect to be asked difficult questions and be prepared to provide answers that display your strength in adversity. And most importantly, be likable and confident throughout the process.

Here are general rules for handling any challenging points in your work history:

- Always focus on the silver lining of any negative situation and explain how you improved as a person because of the experience.
- Describe negative situations as "challenges" and never as "problems."
- Do not say anything negative about anyone. EVER! From a hiring manager's perspective, there are always two sides to a story and somewhere in the middle is the truth. Always be diplomatic. If you speak poorly about a previous boss or co-worker, you can easily be viewed as a future problem/complainer/troublemaker. No employer wants to hire this type of worker.
- When pressed about a negative situation, always weave in what you learned from the situation versus what the other person did wrong and how it affected you.

Here are specific, yet common, situations job seekers face, with guidance on how to handle them fearlessly:

Fired?

If you have been fired, prepare a diplomatic way to convey this and focus on what you learned from the event. An example of how to answer why you left a firm could be something like:

"Management decided the position I held was not the best fit for me and I was released to find a role that was better suited for my skills. I enjoyed working with accounts and ensuring their needs and requests were serviced. This resulted in my producing significant new income from up-selling services. My boss and I thought I would be great at sales since I was already generating a solid income stream. So when a sales position became open, I jumped at the opportunity, even though it was a risk.

"In hindsight, I was not as skilled at cultivating new contacts as I was at nurturing existing relationships, so I struggled with the new position. I attended training and performed countless hours of role-playing on my own time to improve my skills in this area, but I just could not improve to the levels needed to succeed in the role. My previous role was now filled and unavailable to me. So we agreed I would leave my position amicably, as I have no regrets trying something new that challenged me. It also helped me to learn that I really enjoy working with clients on large-scale initiatives, which is why I'm looking to return to that type of role in a larger capacity."

Had a difficult boss?

If you had a difficult boss in your work history, embrace that

STEP 7: MASTER THE INTERVIEW MINDSET TO LAND THE JOB

experience. Don't fight it. Accept that this person came into your life to teach you things about yourself that you did not know and would not have learned otherwise.

With that in mind, ask yourself: what did working for this difficult person teach me about myself? What made them difficult to work for? And what part did I contribute to the conflict? What did I learn about my part and how did I correct my actions? By answering these questions, you can formulate an answer that will position your challenging situation as a growth opportunity.

Here is a sample answer you could give for this common interview question, "Tell me about the most difficult person you worked for in your career."

> "The most challenging person I worked for would probably be ___<insert name here> ___ at ___<Insert company name here> ___. He was difficult to work for because he worked around the clock with exceptionally high standards. While admittedly it was sometimes not pleasant to answer an email on a Saturday morning at 7 am (said with a smile), I understood the importance of responding quickly to our demanding clientele. I was always available to ensure our clients were satisfied. I appreciate the fact that ___<insert name here> ___ was demanding, as I could prove to him and to myself that I can produce quality work in tight time frames under extreme pressure. Before working for him, I did not know that I was capable of that and so I am grateful for that opportunity."

Worked with a less than cooperative co-worker?

The company may want to get a glimpse of how you would deal with colorful characters on their staff. If asked about how you have dealt in the past with challenging co-workers, do not focus on what the person did wrong to you. Describe what you learned from the situation and how you can handle a variety of challenging people.

Here is an example of how you can model the answer:

"Personalities are going to vary within staffs and I fully accept that. While I aim to get along with everyone, I realize situations can arise where people may not like me or my work style. If this happens, and luckily it does not happen often, I aim to stick to the work issue at hand and not engage in any personal commentary that can be misconstrued. I ensure that deadlines, directions and deliverables are clear on both sides and get the project qualitatively off my plate as quickly as possible. I don't look to be right in confrontational situations; I try to advocate for items that are in the company's best interest."

If you are actually asked about a specific person and pinned to discuss it, be cautiously diplomatic. Do not think the best answer is giving the interviewer the dirt they seem to want to hear. It can be a trap to see if you fall for it and let your guard down. So, again, stick to what you learned versus gossiping about anyone else.

Here is an example:

"Yes, working with accounting and business operations as a creative professional can be a challenge, since what is creatively demanded in the marketplace may not always be the most cost-effective solution. This was particularly true of the CFO of our company. He stuck strictly to the numbers and did not factor in any information that was not quantified or documented by research. I was frustrated at times, but I did not fight it. Because of his consistent position, I have become an expert on the business of my craft. While you might not want me as your CFO (said with a smile), I now give rational information backed up by research and examples to support any creative option that I'm advocating. My CFO's challenging position has made me a better creative leader."

Experienced market share loss, client departures, or sales/profit decreases in the past 3 to 5 years?

If you have experienced business losses, you probably do not want to brag about them, but you should not avoid discussing them if asked. Any obvious avoidance or lack of details will suggest there is more to the story and this will arouse suspicion. If you address the losses head-on, you'll leave the interviewer satisfied without having over-answered the question.

Getting a question about business losses is an opportunity to show how you turned a negative situation around or what you learned to prevent it from happening again. Here is one way to position the adverse event:

> "When we lost the Carbide account, it was a setback for our company and for our group. But we used it as a starting point to further examine our client list and uncover our vulnerable spots. I was able to provide data to the controller and sales manager that showed we were too heavily involved in this segment. The data sparked an initiative by the executive team to further diversify the prospects our sales team targeted. This enabled our company to halt the revenue loss it was experiencing and was the beginning of the turnaround."

Small or significant gap in employment?

Acknowledge and be prepared to discuss any gap in your

employment. Having a recent employment gap does not carry the stigma it once did. However, simply expecting the interviewer to understand that these are hard times will not get you far. You need to discuss your time off positively. How you handled your unexpected gap may signal to the employer how self-motivated you are and how you direct your time when not reporting to someone, regardless of your career level.

Here are tools for framing any gap you may have in your career history:

A small gap in employment (defined here as a period under six months) is not a cause for major alarm. Looking for a job is a full-time job in these times. Show that you were engaged in your job search 35-40 hours per week for those few months; provide specifics on your activities, and outline what you learned about yourself, and this should suffice for most interviewers.

If you experienced a significant gap in employment (defined here as over six months), be prepared to discuss what you did during that period besides your job search.

Here is a sampling of my clients' activities during extended periods without full-time employment:

- Consulting work as a 1099 or through a third-party firm
- Research into franchise opportunities
- Exploration of entrepreneurial ventures
- Volunteer activities at professionally related non-profit groups
- Community service volunteer opportunities
- Personal educational and professional development initiatives
- Athletic events (advanced marathons or other elite training activities)
- World or domestic travel

STEP 7: MASTER THE INTERVIEW MINDSET TO LAND THE JOB

- New professional internships (paid and unpaid)

Use these difficult times to position yourself as someone who faces challenges with grace and a positive attitude. Candidates who answer timidly or awkwardly may get tossed aside. Instead, prepare for the hard questions and answer them with foresight and confidence. This will help you differentiate yourself from other candidates.

SPECIAL INTERVIEW SITUATIONS

Certain interview situations can challenge even the most experienced and savvy interviewee. When you're on any kind of interview, *never drop your corporate demeanor*. Avoid being inappropriately casual, especially if your interviewer is extremely friendly or overly casual. Do not follow their lead and lose your corporate front.

This is not to say don't be friendly. But always remember there's a difference between treating the interviewer cordially and amicably, and treating the person like you've been best friends since high school. This is still an interview, and the interviewer has the job at the firm—you do not.

Always keep your interview guard up. Be conscious of your conduct during these situations:

- When out to lunch or dinner with the interviewer, act respectfully to all restaurant employees and to anyone you encounter on the way to or from the restaurant.
- Do not talk negatively about anyone. The interviewer may gossip, but you should never, ever lose sight of the fact that you are in an interview.

- Beware of situations with alcohol. Never have more than one drink, if any. Never over-indulge, even if employees of the firm do—if you over-indulge slightly, you will not be hired.

HOW TO NAIL PHONE INTERVIEWS

A phone interview is an interview. Period. Make no mistake: it is not a pre-interview, an informal conversation or a brief, preliminary chat. The interview clock starts the minute you send your resume to the company or receive a call from someone who saw your LinkedIn profile, and it is certainly ticking during a phone interview.

Prepare for this type of interview the same way you would for any other interview. If you receive the call unexpectedly, step up to the role of the interviewee as best you can in the moment. You may not get another shot. Do all you can to answer the phone if it is an unplanned call. But if you are truly in a place where you cannot speak, then let it go to voice mail and take your chances calling back.

For planned interview calls, there are special steps you can take to ensure you make the best impression:

- **Get dressed for the call** as you would for the in-person interview. If you do not want to put a full suit on, dress conservatively for the phone interview. Even though no-one will see you, you will be more on your game if you're dressed for business.
- **Ensure you have strong phone reception**, with little or no background noise.

STEP 7: MASTER THE INTERVIEW MINDSET TO LAND THE JOB

- **Make sure your environment is quiet** and will not cause distractions during your call. Eliminate visual and audible distractions.
- **Try very hard to avoid the use of a speakerphone** by either you or the interviewer.
- **Be animated and speak in as natural a manner as possible.** Display energy in your voice. In a regular interview, you have your gestures, body language, attire, and facial expressions to help convey your enthusiasm. On a phone interview, all you have is your voice to convey your spirit and enthusiasm. Focus on using your tone, pitch and words to convey your excitement about the role. I often tell clients, if it feels a little unnatural and uncomfortable for you, then you are probably doing it right.
- **Answer yes or no questions using one to three sentences.** The dialogue will be more conversational this way and more comfortable for both of you.
- **Do not multi-task** while you are on the phone. This means no reading emails, no texting, no housework, no chores, no driving, and no web browsing—unless it is to look up something said in the interview. Give your full attention to your call.
- **Smile** when answering the phone. It is said that one can "hear" a smile over the phone.
- **Take notes** during the interview—even more than you would during a normal interview. no-one can see if you write a lot. Be sure to reference the notes you've taken during the interview to show solid listening skills, good recall abilities, and adept application skills.

SUCCESSFUL VIDEO INTERVIEWING TIPS FOR JOB SEEKERS

Employers are using video for interviewing more than ever to save time and money. No need to fly candidates in or schedule all-day interviews to capitalize on a candidate physically being in town. With an increasing global workforce where teams work remotely, video interviewing helps to see how a candidate interfaces virtually as a precursor to how they will communicate virtually with a team.

Companies typically use video for the initial screening interview. However, I have seen entire hiring processes done virtually to make a hire. How they use video during the interview process depends on the structure of the company and what the company is trying to assess.

Here are some successful video interviewing tips that can help you impress your prospective employer and allow your strengths to resonate with the hiring manager:

1. Remember, **everyone thinks these types of interviews are awkward.** It's not just you. Every job seeker is relatively new at interviewing via one-way video or a video conference call, so all you have to do is to be better than your competition, who also is uncomfortable doing this type of interview. This is a new way to communicate, and it's a skill we need to acquire.
2. **Practice by making a video of yourself** answering sample interview questions—then watch yourself answering the questions on camera. That is what you will most likely look like on the screen to the interviewer. Make note of adjustments, mannerisms,

STEP 7: MASTER THE INTERVIEW MINDSET TO LAND THE JOB

eye contact, and background settings when applying these successful video interviewing tips.

3. **Treat video interviews like a regular interview**—so prepare as if it was a regular in-person interview. Do your research on the company, interviewer, job, and yourself, like you normally would for an in-person or phone interview.
4. **Be yourself**—on a physical interview, you would engage in small talk, have casual conversation, and allow the interviewer to get to know you as a person. Do not let the technology get in the way of this happening. People hire people they like and those with the skills—so focus on being likeable through the technology.
5. **Do not lose sight of the formality** of this meeting, especially if your video interview is happening at home with your webcam. Silence all pets, leave a sign on your front door to not be disturbed, and turn off phone ringers. If you have to go to an office, get there early to allow time to get settled, see how you present on their camera, and possibly do a trial run to test the equipment.
6. **Look at your background**—is it disorganized or professional? Consider taking down some family pictures in the background and balance it out by hanging your college degree. Do you have inappropriate or awkward items within the interviewer's sight? Be sure to put forth a clean, professional image by making sure the background is free of visual distractions.
7. **Fully dress for the call**—yes, wear your suit pants and not your comfy Hawaiian shorts with your collared

shirt and suit jacket. You may not think they will see your legs, but if you need to get up for any reason during the interview, can you say, "Awkward?"

8. **Dress in solid colors.** Video is not the time for that fabulous, new print tie or striped collared shirt—prints and patterns can overpower the screen and make it hard for the interviewer to watch you. It can also detract from what you're saying—and that is the whole point of the interview, yes?

9. **Video interviewing can leave an impression—**literally. Often employers record the interviews to compare your answers to other candidates. So be sure that what you're sharing in the interview is something you're okay with being recorded.

10. **Put on your best newscaster face.** On video and phone interviews, you have to be a little more animated and expressive than you would be in person to convey your enthusiasm. If you feel you are a little too happy, chances are you're probably doing it right. Test yourself by filming yourself answering some sample questions to see what it looks like.

Video is not the wave of the future—it is already here. We all have to embrace it and work at doing it successfully. With the successful video interviewing tips above, you are certain to have a solid chance to edge out your competition.

Is there any difference between a two-way video interview and an in-person interview?

Some say relationship building is more robust in an in-person interview, but logistics are the main difference. In a video

STEP 7: MASTER THE INTERVIEW MINDSET TO LAND THE JOB

interview, be conscious of your background and noises in your environment. Ensure your internet connection is solid and have a technical backup plan (landline, mobile, Google Voice). Remember employers often record interviews to compare answers, so make sure you're okay with everything you say being recorded. These are not necessarily causes for concern in an in-person interview.

Treat video interviews like a regular interview—prepare as if it was a regular in-person interview. Do your research on the company, interviewer, job and yourself, like you normally would for an in-person or phone interview.

Preparing for a video interview is very similar to preparing for an in-person interview.

I believe the interview, and a video interview is no different, can present opportunities on how the candidate reacts to difficulties or unexpected activities that occur. For instance, if you experience technical difficulties during the call, offer to call using a landline or cell phone. Google chat may be a viable option. I would suggest rescheduling as a last option only if trying another medium doesn't work. Seeing how a candidate reacts to adversity during the interview indicates how fluid the candidate is when things do not go as planned.

We work with our executive clients on communication delivery as well as interview research for being prepared for the interview. The main point we focus on is to prepare the candidate for various lines of questioning about themselves, how they will respond in a situation, and demonstrations of critical thinking in business scenarios.

Most candidates make the mistake of studying the company and competitors, but not themselves. Companies will ask mainly about you and your thoughts, so our successful candidates spend most of the interview prep time studying themselves and thinking through situations to respond to as practice. This premise is important, no matter what medium is used for the interview.

BE ARMED FOR THE "DO YOU HAVE ANY QUESTIONS FOR US?" QUESTION

Your questions should not only come at the end of the interview when they ask this classic question. Be prepared with questions you can pose throughout the interview.

In some interviews, the interviewer starts by asking you for questions to determine your interest, evaluate what you already know, insert you into a stressful situation, and see how you think on your feet.

They will ask you things like:

- What do you know about us?
- What do you know about this job?
- Why do you want this job?

If this happens to you, answer the question with a sentence or two, then ask a related question that can provide you with insights for the rest of the interview. Ask a question like one of these at the beginning of the interview, if you get the opportunity:

- What issues are you hoping to address or problems are you looking to solve by hiring someone in this position?
- What interested you about my background and showed that I may have what you are seeking in the next hire?

Throughout the interview, it is imperative to come across as interested and inquisitive. An interactive discussion makes things

STEP 7: MASTER THE INTERVIEW MINDSET TO LAND THE JOB

easier for you and the interviewer. So be prepared to ask for more detail or further explanations. Effective ways to do this include:

- "That certainly sounds like a different approach. Can you expand upon how the team is addressing that idea?"
- "Can you tell me more about that situation?"
- "How did the team rectify that issue?"

If you feel you must ask questions at the end of the interview, aim to have questions that reference items you discussed throughout the interview, in addition to questions that bring out new information. Some examples are:

- "What challenges will the person experience in the first 90 days of this position? What about the long-term?"
- "Who would I be interacting with most within the first 90 days of hire?"

Ask for performance information on products and services if this information is not publicly available. If those numbers are publicly available, ask about decisions being made that can affect the future performance of those numbers.

Reference recent news about the firm in a question: "Congratulations on the firm landing a place in the Top 100 Best Places to Work listing. As outlined by the article, the firm is doing a lot of things right. What specifically makes people excited to work here, do you think?"

Ask for opinions and background information from the interviewer to gain understanding about the firm. "I understand you've been here a while. That is commendable. What is the company doing right to keep you here?" Or if the interviewer is a new hire, "What about the company attracted you here and made you choose to work here?"

Other questions include:

- "Of the employees who are successful within the company, what common traits would you say they exhibit?"
- "If you find an employee does not work out, have you observed a specific reason in common why it was not a good match?"

In fact, if the interview is a more of a dialogue and less an inquisition, you may find you've asked all your questions during the interview and they've been satisfactorily answered. What do you then say if asked for questions at the end of this type of conversation? Use something like:

"Thank you for asking this. You thoroughly answered all of my questions throughout our discussion, making me even more excited to continue in this process of consideration. Do you have any additional questions for me?"

WHAT NOT TO ASK ON A FIRST INTERVIEW

Virtually all the things not to ask on a first interview are in the "What's in it for me?" category, otherwise known as the WIIFM questions. Items that qualify for this category are questions about:

- Salary
- Time-off policies (sick days, vacation, etc.)
- Disability and FMLA policies
- Bonus and performance raises

- Employee perks and discounts
- Healthcare benefits
- Retirement plans and matches
- Education reimbursement

You want to spend the interview discussing why you're the best fit for the role. If you prove that, there will be plenty of time to discuss what the firm offers. And by waiting until they express interest, you typically gain better leverage to get what you want.

AFTER THE INTERVIEW—THANK-YOU NOTES AND FOLLOWING UP

After the first interview and after any subsequent interviews, send personal thank-you notes to each person who interviewed you. Do this to express your gratitude and display your excitement for the role.

Write a personal note to each person you interviewed with, and send it within 24 hours of the interview. Even if it was a group interview, where you were interviewed by several people, sending a custom note to each person is not just a nice touch, but an essential step.

Gather business cards from every person you speak with during the interview. This will help ensure accuracy with name spellings and titles.

Reference parts of the conversation to show solid listening skills for each thank-you note sent.

Reiterate your interest in the position. If needed, provide supplemental information to reinforce your candidacy.

Email is now an acceptable way to send a thank-you note, as long as you send it within 24 hours of the interview. Email is even a preferred means of sending the note, because of the speed of the interview process.

If you need to send a thank-you note via snail mail, I suggest you mail it by overnight mail to impress the interviewer with the strength of your interest. If other candidates are promptly emailing thank-you notes and your mailed note comes in two or three days later, you can lose out in comparison.

Have someone read your note before sending to ensure no spelling or grammatical errors.

If the interviewer mentions they will get back to you in a week, give it 7-10 business days for your next follow-up. At that point, send an email that reiterates your interest and indicates that you are aiming to stay top of mind for the position. Tell them you know they will get back to you as soon as they have new information, but you are just staying on their radar.

This approach is respectful but assertive, without making the interviewer feel harassed.

HANDLING THE SALARY QUESTION AND WHEN TO DO SO

As a search firm recruiter, I would handle salary negotiations on behalf of the candidate. If you're working with a search firm recruiter, allow them to broker the terms on your behalf so you can focus your own discussions on outlining how you are the best fit for the job.

But what if you're dealing with the company directly? When do you bring up the money question to ensure you're not wasting your time? If the company is qualifying candidates correctly and asking for salary requirements, I can assure you that you are being interviewed because you meet their minimum job qualifications and you are within their budgeted salary. In these cases, you can

STEP 7: MASTER THE INTERVIEW MINDSET TO LAND THE JOB

focus on proving to the employer that you are the best person for the role.

If the company does not qualify candidates with a salary requirement question, then one of two things is most likely happening:

1. They are truly flexible in compensation, within the market standards for the position. They might pay above market rate for the best talent. You then want to show not only that you are qualified, but that you are worthy of the high-end of their compensation package.
2. The employer is unsophisticated in its recruitment practices. They may not realize that asking for salary requirements ensures that neither the candidate nor the company wastes time. Or they do this purposefully to see whether the candidate will fall in love with the job during the interview—and then accept a low-ball offer. This lack of sophistication can help you determine if this is a place where you want to work, and if you do, that you go into it fully aware of your reasons and terms.

What if they ask about your salary needs in the interview—and in the first interview at that? If they ask about your salary requirements at any point during the interview process, even on the first interview, answer the question. Don't avoid it or circumvent it with a passive answer. After all, you're not looking to volunteer with this company. You're looking to make a living doing something you love that enables the company to meet its goals. So don't be shy about your salary requirements, but be graceful, matter-of-fact, and professional in delivering your answer.

If asked about your previous compensation, outline your total compensation number, including salary, bonuses, value of benefits, etc. Make no excuses for your salary—it is what it is.

If asked about your salary history, state your previous salaries, specifying what the bases were, plus the bonuses and benefits. I recommend not answering a question about base salary with a total compensation number, but state the salary with an indication of the other numbers separately.

Don't discuss your financial situation at all. If you need the money or not is not the issue at hand. You want the recruiter/hiring manager to focus on your qualifications for the job. If the candidate was in their twenties, they would not focus on whether they were on their own or living with their parents. So as an experienced, over 40+ candidate, whether your kids are out of college and you do not need as much money as you did before, has no bearing on whether you are qualified at the market rate for that job. Don't bring it up.

If they ask what you're looking for in your next role, realize this is a very different question from asking what you made in past jobs. Granted, what you're looking for must be in line with your skills and what the market demands. Assuming you have those elements in line, you can answer the question in the following manner:

> "I am interviewing for roles in the low 70s to high 70s salary range and I am flexible based on the nature of the responsibilities for the position."

Let's pull this apart:

"I am interviewing for...." – this phrase is better than "I am looking for..." or "I want..." First, no-one really cares what you are looking for or what you want. What the prospective employer wants to know is, are your expectations realistic and are you worth

STEP 7: MASTER THE INTERVIEW MINDSET TO LAND THE JOB

it? Saying "I am interviewing for..." implies that companies are calling you to interview for that role, so your intrinsic worth is implied and reinforced.

"**...in the low 70s to high 70s salary range...**"—outlining a fuzzy range versus using hard numbers sends a message of flexibility in your candidacy. It allows you to be flexible while still enabling the employer to feel good about an offer they may present to you. If you were to give your range as "...in the 73K to 77K range..." and the company wants to offer you 72K, you have just put them in a position of thinking you might be disappointed with their offer. No employer wants to make an offer that is disappointing to their new hire. However, if you had said low 70s, an offer at 72K is well within that scope. On the flip side, if they wanted to offer you 79K, by saying high 70s, they may offer you 79K. If stated 73K to 77K, I can assure you they will most likely offer you 77K, causing you to lose 2K.

"**...and I am flexible based on the nature of the responsibilities for the position.**"—tacking this phrase at the end of your salary requirement will enable you to back-pedal somewhat gracefully if you misunderstood the demands of the role or you were not fully informed about its duties. If you learn there is more responsibility involved, you can indicate that your initial salary requirement was for a less responsible role. Or, if it seems the role is not as demanding as you thought, you can indicate that you would accept a lower range for a role without senior responsibilities. It is not guaranteed that your graceful back-pedaling will win over the interviewer, but without attempting it, you almost certainly won't be considered any further.

CONCLUSION
GO OUT THERE AND LAND A JOB THAT MAKES YOU HAPPY!

Looking for a new job can feel very daunting, especially if you attempt it without a plan. This book has given you the 7 steps you need:

1. Define the job you want (and the job you don't want)
2. Evaluate your resume
3. Ensure your LinkedIn profile measures up
4. Create a Powerful Resume and LinkedIn profile
5. Create effective cover letters and career communications
6. Design and execute your personalized job landing plan
7. Master the interview mindset to land the job

Follow these 7 steps, and you now have a full range of tools and insights to help you successfully navigate the admittedly stressful interviewing process.

Embrace your current situation and make a commitment to applying the tools in this book—and position yourself to interview confidently and land a rewarding job on your terms.

Contact Chameleon Resumes to inquire about personalized support that can help you with your resume branding, job search activities, and ongoing career development:

Visit: www.chameleonresumes.com

Email: support@chameleonresumes.com

We wish you much success!

NEXT STEPS

Want personalized resume writing and job search services to advance your job search that much faster?

Invest in our Ultimate Job Search Plan

www.chameleonresumes.com/ultimate-job-search

Get 120-minutes of one-on-one coaching time to use however you wish plus the following ways:

- Create your resume and LinkedIn profile then get it critiqued by a recruiter/job landing coach.
- Get job landing tactics and best practices from a sought-after recruiter who found candidates.
- Ensure your resume and LinkedIn profile have an aligned message so you don't get rejected for an interview you're qualified for.
- Get access to the cover letter and thank you note secret sauce that can help you land the interview and seal the deal.

Take the mystery out of finding hiring managers and figuring out what to say by learning how to connect with hard-to-find recruiters and get call backs. You can make this easier and faster by asking our expert team. We are always here for you to call through our Ultimate Job Search Plan.

BUY NOW:

www.chameleonresumes.com/ultimate-job-search

APPENDIX 1
SAMPLE POWERFUL RESUMES

APPENDIX 1

SAMPLE RESUME #1 – Technology Professional – Employment Gap to Update Skills

FirstName LastName
123 Main Street, City, State 01234
youremail@provider.com | www.linkedin.com/in/firstnamelastname
444.555.1380

SOLUTIONS-DRIVEN SYSTEMS ANALYST
*Small Business & Corporate Expertise | Detailed Project Coordinator & Facilitator
Effective End-User & Technical Team Communication Liaison*

Experienced IT problem solver with a history of projects utilizing database design techniques for professional services environments. Additionally, possess corporate achievements demonstrating project management and persuasive communication skills to devise and execute solutions for production, banking, and marketing functions. Advanced interpersonal and business communication skills with the ability to be the communication bridge between end-users and technology staff. Adept at defining client needs, designing solutions and implementing application plans effectively. Exceptional diagnostic and troubleshooting skills that can rectify most technical issues.

- Business Analysis & Process Flow
- System Architecture & Database Development
- Client & Internal User Needs Assessment
- Specification Gathering & Writing
- End-User / Client Training & Help Desk Assistance
- Diplomatic Communication & Facilitation Skills

TECHNICAL SKILLS
Database Management Systems: MS SQL, Oracle, MySQL, Paradox
Languages: Python, Java, JavaScript, PHP, VB.Net, HTML, XHTML, CSS

PREVIOUS CLIENTS & EMPLOYERS
CompTech Packaging, Tishman Speyer, Kraft, First Union Bank, Hastings LLC, Schick, Victoria's Secret, Liz Claiborne

PROFESSIONAL/TECHNICAL SQL SKILL DEVELOPMENT SABBATICAL, Bridgewater, NJ — 2015 – present
- Successfully completed the nine-week Python Programming Program from Targeted Focus, a project training program within simulated work environments using programming, analysis and design skills to devise corporate IT solutions.
- Served as project team leader to design a management information system for a multi-location business. Delegated development stored procedures, XML functions, database design, indexing, tuning and maintenance to team members.
- Developed prototype to create a membership database for 3200-member roster of the Insurance Professionals Group.

DBA / DATABASE DEVELOPER, CompTech Packaging, Piscataway, NJ — 2012 – 2015
- Designed, developed and implemented a fully integrated ERP system for this $18 Million, privately-held, co-packing facility that assembled products from manufacturers, such as Liz Claiborne, Victoria's Secret and Schick.
- Reduced labor costs by $225/hr and increased profit margins by creating systems that tracked materials from receipt through shipment and allowed for quicker responses to customer requests.
- Devised concise, multilingual GUI for the ERP system and implemented secure internet access to the ERP system.
- Hired and trained four interns to support 250-person staff (seasonal and year-round staff) and worked directly with users to understand needs and develop appropriate solutions.
- Served as the sole IT employee and interfaced successfully with shipping/receiving clerks, transportation drivers, production staff, executive management, sales employees and accounting professionals regarding IT needs and client interfaces.

APPENDIX 1

FirstName LastName – page 2   123.567.6789 | prefix@domain.com

FOUNDER – LEAD PROGRAMMER & DESIGNER, ParaSoft, Inc., Basking Ridge, NJ   2009 – 2012

- Created and implemented information management systems with database techniques for clients, such as, Bank Julius Baer, Connell Company, Kraft, Tishman Speyer, in manufacturing, banking, marketing, leasing and real estate industries.
- Coordinated and directed teams of up to eight consultants, provided detailed project specifications, tracked progress on multiple concurrent projects and effectively balanced time and customer requirements.
- Worked with managers and end users to clarify and refine requirements to align project designs to satisfy business needs.
- Demonstrated solid technical planning skills and utilized sound problem solving capabilities in coordinating cross-industry projects with budgets ranging from $33,000 to $144,000.
- Led team to develop a financial reporting system for a manufacturing company under budget and ahead of schedule.
- Replaced a team of four consultants over a 12-week project (estimated project savings: $57,000) to provide strategic consulting to a marketing organization that enabled them to win a $1.5 Million pharmaceutical client contract. Subsequently hired to develop an automated solution to fill the requirements of the contract.
- Served as the key contributor to a team project to develop a stock-broker trading system for a financial services client.
- Designed and developed a mortgage-backed securities portfolio analysis system for Bank Julius Baer, a major Swiss bank.
- Contributed key segments to a tax lien system that generated an additional $400,000/month in collected receivables for First Union National Bank, a large regional bank which has since merged with Wachovia Bank.

EDUCATION

TargetedFocus LLC, Fort Lee, NJ - *SQL Master's Program*

Bergen County Community College, Montclair, NJ - *Certificate, Web Programming, with honors*

Villanova University, Villanova, PA - *Bachelor of Science, Business Administration*

APPENDIX 1

SAMPLE RESUME #2 – Mid-Level Sales Manager
FIRSTNAME LASTNAME
123 Main Street, City, State, Zip
123.567.6789 | prefix@domain.com
linkedin.com/in/firstnamelastname

RESULTS-PRODUCING SALES TEAM DIRECTOR

Accomplished Sales Director who exceeds revenue objectives though focused business development, effective pipeline management and qualitative mentorship. Established sales leader who consistently secures business within Fortune 500 firms and niche areas. Trains top performers on needs assessment and diplomatic negotiation skills that generate results.

PROMINENT ADVERTISING FIRM, San Francisco, CA   March 2012 – present
Sales Director (6/2014 – present)
- Manage most profitable sales team that generated $34 Million in annual profits in 2014(108% of plan).
- Develop business and manage partnerships with F500 and government clients from various industries, such as UPS, General Electric, Citigroup, Morgan Stanley, The Home Depot, Pfizer and Walt Disney.
- Partner with the Vice President of Sales and Marketing to set strategy and devise plans to achieve goals.
- Developed five President Club Achievers and promoted four through targeted performance planning.
- Evaluate team performance and document development plans to optimize results and eliminate low performing employees. Proactively interview sales candidates to select high caliber new staff.
- Perform weekly sales meetings to produce accurate forecasts and to recalibrate plans as needed.
- Lead product meetings and demonstrate sales tactics to enable team to meet corporate objectives.

Accounts Sales Manager (4/2013 – 6/2014)
- Managed ten Account Representatives responsible for F1000 accounts with revenues of $15 Million.
- Negotiated enterprise contracts, sales forecasting, training and high level client presentations.
- Achieved President's Club in 2006 for managing team to exceed production quota (104% of quota).

Account Executive (3/2012 – 3/2013)
- Generated new business through working with clients to create strategic advertising campaigns.
- Demonstrated ROI to key decision makers and up sold products based on detailed needs assessment.
- Ranked #1 nationally of 24 and only person to achieve over 100% of 2006 goal (achieved 110% of goal).
- Achieved President's Club for 1st half and 2nd half of 2006.

NATIONAL SERVICES FIRM, New York, NY   December 2007 – February 2012
Field Services Supervisor
- Managed 120 delivery staff in a union environment handling scheduling, coaching and evaluation.
- Performed extensive logistical work to forecast and planned deliveries to ensure maximum productivity.
- Provided timely technical expertise in escalated problem solving, decision making and service issues.

EDUCATION   Pennsylvania State University, B.S. Business Administration – GPA 3.84/4.00   2007

APPENDIX 1

FirstName LastName
123 Main Street, City, State, Zip
123.567.6789 | prefix@domain.com

PRIVATE EQUITY EXECUTIVE LEADER

*Orchestrating International Buyouts and Securing Growth Capital
for Global Telecommunication and Communication Investments*

Founder of an international private equity investment partnership focused on operationally intensive telecommunications, media, and technology services opportunities. Pursing large-scale emerging markets opportunities worldwide to apply extensive experience of investing in, developing, and exiting from businesses in mainstream markets in the US, Russia, Europe, and the Middle East. Possess a precise combination of investment instinct, traditional private equity skills, execution track record, and top level business contacts worldwide.

- Partner-Level Private Equity Experience
- Three Successful Exits
- Two Foreign Office Launches
- Public & Private Company Board Expertise

- Extensive Deal Sourcing & Construction
- Mergers, Acquisitions & Debt Restructuring
- Fluent in Arabic, Spanish, and Russian
- US Government Financing Relationships

ROYAL PINNACLE CAPITAL, New York, NY   2015 – Present
Global private equity partnership focused on investments in telecommunications, media, and technology sectors in emerging markets.
Founder, Managing Partner
- Built core team of four partners, developed investment holding and management company structures, established fund administration processes, and opened the Moscow satellite office.
- Source, execute and manage a portfolio of seven growth investments in target sectors in EMEA.
- Serve as Chairman of the Board of Directors of firm's man investment, **Galaxy Networks**, a leading Moscow broadband Internet service provider with over 400,000 customer home subscribers.
    o Execute a comprehensive restructuring resulting in an eight-fold increase in cash flow after two quarters.
    o Restructure and refinance outstanding debt obligations securing a $28 million loan facility from a U.S. Treasury affiliate to fund the Galaxy Network's service provider strategy.
    o Complete acquisitions of two competitors and fully integrate their operations into the firm.
- Lead firm's growth investment in **Manony Communications**, a leading Middle Eastern cable TV broadcaster, which operates eight mainstream entertainment channels.
    o Expand into the Middle East by acquiring and launching a Saudi children's television channel.

MOSKUS CAPITAL, Moscow, Russia / New York, NY   2011 – 2015
US private equity firm with $2 billion of capital under management, a division of Nova Group, managed by the notable Peter Meklesburg.
Partner, Head of Moscow Office
- Established the Moscow office, investment holding, company structures, and the 27-person team.
- Served as President/CFO of the group's media/telecoms consolidation vehicle, **Nova Group Enterprises**.
- Served as an **Independent Director** and **Member of the Audit Committee** until Firm was taken private through a negotiated tender offer following the merger.

FirstName LastName, page 2   123.567.6789 | prefix@domain.com

APPENDIX 1

- Executed $42 million investment in NASDAQ-listed **Petersburg Cablecom** (Moscow's largest cable TV operator) and served as a Member of Board of Directors and Chairman of its operating subsidiary.
    - Installed a new management team, capitalized an aggressive growth plan, and oversaw execution that resulted in a four-fold network expansion and an attainment of profitability.
- Participated in the $735 million acquisition of 31% of **RuskCom** (Russian state's telecom holding) from Ford Capital and the $146 million LBO of **Aspire Networks** from US Telecom.
- Originated and led a $354 million cash and stock merger creating **Kitoda**, the largest cable TV operator in Moscow. Realized an **exit of 108% IRR by entering into the merger**.

AMERICAVON CAPITAL, London, UK   2007 – 2011
US-based private equity firm with $20 billion of capital under management, investing primarily in buyout and recapitalization opportunities in upper middle-market companies in Europe and North America.
Senior Associate - *Western European Telecoms & Business Services Buyout Team*
- Sourced and executed firm's **$100 million LBO of Paybourg**, a Luxembourg provider of billing services.
    - Arranged $50 million in financing for the buyout from Deutsche Bank, Bank of Scotland, and Allianz.
    - Assembled the strongest team in the sector from IMF Billing Structures, the leading competitor.
    - Led financial restructuring of Paybourg corporate structure post-buyout.
    - Americanvon **realized a 115% IRR upon exit from Paybourg** into another private equity firm in 2005.
- Participated in $950 million LBO of SpainTel (joint venture between Telecom Spain and Network Systems) and the $72 million equity investment in Ataltel (Italian broadband communications service provider).
- Sourced Americavon's investment in **Oxycom International** (Swiss-based provider of network planning and OSS optimization services for IP and cellular networks).

EXPLORGOLD INTERNATIONAL, London, UK   1997 – 2007
Leading financial services firm with a market capitalization of $70.4 billion and a presence in every major financial market worldwide.
Associate/Analyst - *Investment Banking*
- Executed all major types of M&A and financing transactions in chemicals, transportation, telecommunications, and travel management sectors worldwide, including:
    - $36 billion acquisition of UK cellular operator **RedCell Communications** by Vediorsan NV.
    - $600 million follow-on equity offerings by **Bangalore Air**, India's largest low-fare airline.
    - M&A advisory work with Alitalia, Knightsbridge Tankers, Logica, Permira, Philips and Thomas Cook.
    - Participated in the 1999 IPO of **Exploragold International, Inc.**

TERING BROTHERS, **Investment Banking Analyst**, London, UK   1994 – 1997
HAMILTON & ROGERS, **Researcher / Legal Assistant**, New York, NY 1991 – 1994

FORD BUSINESS SCHOOL, New York, NY   Expected completion 2018
Candidate for Master of Business Administration (Executive MBA Program)

AARON BURR COLLEGE, Carter, NY   1995
Bachelor of Arts with Honors in Philosophy

L'INSTITUT D'ÉTUDES POLITIQUES DE PARIS (SCIENCES-PO), Paris, France   1994
European Studies Semester

RUSSIAN STATE INSTITUTE OF INTERNATIONAL RELATIONS (MGIMO), Moscow, Russia   1991

APPENDIX 1

FIRSTNAME LASTNAME
123 Main Street, City, State, Zip
123.567.6789 | prefix@domain.com | http://linkedin/in/vanityurl

HUMAN RESOURCES ADMINISTRATOR

Returning-to-Work Human Resources Administrator with broad experience coordinating all facets of human resources and supporting HR executives within for-profit and non-profit organizations. Create and implement programs within challenging financial constraints for performance-driven and client-focused organizations. Proven track record in providing guidance to managers through accelerated growth phases and turbulent economic periods.. Committed to local communities through volunteer leadership.

- Human Resources Planning Implementation
- Benefit Administration & Compensation
- Employee Relations, Retention & Engagement
- New Hire Training and Staff Development
- HR Policy Design & Administration
- Employer Branding & Community Relations
- Leadership & Executive Development
- Professional & Staff Level Recruitment

RELATED VOLUNTEER EXPERIENCE

City Institute of Art, Dallas, TX, *Board Member & Co-Chair* 2014 – present
- Developed strong relationships with entertainment, city and corporate leaders to support fundraising.

Children's Organization of America, Dallas, TX *Chairperson* 2013 – present
- Given an award for raising the most money (over $200,000 in one year) in the history of the organization
- Developed corporate sponsors, recruited community donations and launched various fundraising events

Cultural Group Fund, *Event Chairperson for "Summer Soiree"*
- Chaired elite event coordinating volunteers to raised $450,000+ at one dinner with more than 500 guests.

Society for Human Resources Management - *Current Member* 2013 – present

HUMAN RESOURCES EXPERIENCE

Versatile Hospital, Dallas, TX 2006 – 2012
Director of Human Resources
- Created, managed and administered HR policies and programs for a 200-bed community hospital
- Developed infrastructure for operations and directed departments with a $2.7 Million operational budget
- Wrote 62 job descriptions for all hospital positions and developed related training and operating manuals
- Conduct training programs to improve performance and develop advancements for 175- employee workforce
- Established health benefit cafeteria plans through complex contract negotiations with third party vendors
- Negotiated the 401K plan contract with Merrill Lynch that kept service the same at a 14% reduced fee
- Served as employee relations liaison between hospital and staff to resolve employee disputes and issues

County Municipality, Dallas, TX 2002 – 2006
Manager - Employee Benefits Department
- Implemented and managed health benefit and COBRA programs for 5000+ employees and 11,000+ retirees
- Led project to automate employment records that resulted in a $457,000 annual labor cost savings
- Handled salary administration with 558 managers by reviewing employee ratings, job skills and tenure

EDUCATION

MARYGROVE UNIVERSITY, DETROIT, MI - *Master of Science*: Business Administration & Human Resources
UNIVERSITY OF MARYLAND, COLLEGE PARK, MD - *Bachelor of Science*: Business Administration

APPENDIX 1

FirstName LastName
City, State
123.465.7811 | prefix@domain.com
http://linkedin/in/vanityurl

PRODUCT DEVELOPMENT MANAGER

Geographical & Cultural Team Integration | Product Development & Execution

Global Product Development Manager who conceptualizes, designs and produces progressive-minded products that exceed client needs, increase IMU, optimize revenues and generate buzz within multiple product categories.

Business-savvy designer and resourceful thinker with an intuitively, sophisticated style who inspires teams to create products within guidelines that supersede corporate objectives. Streamlined full-cycle development practices that have delivered production on time and within budget consistently.

- ✓ *Inventive Product Design & Development*
- ✓ *Vendor, Client & Press Relations*
- ✓ *Product Sourcing & Contract Negotiations*
- ✓ *Wholesale & Retail Distribution & Buying*
- ✓ *Public Relations & Published Designs*
- ✓ *Strategic Marketing Development*
- ✓ *Growth & Established Brand Expertise*
- ✓ *Fiscal, Costing & Talent Management*

PROFESSIONAL EXPERIENCE

C.E.F. LLC | Los Angeles, CA   October 2012 – Present

Private label evening dress company with $4 Million in revenues located in Los Angeles, NYC and Hong Kong that received global publicity in leading fashion publications, such as Vogue, Cosmopolitan and Women's Wear Daily.

Product Development Manager

- Formulated a business plan, obtained financing and leveraged extensive, global contact base to launch the design and marketing functions in NJ/NYC and a production in Asia.
- Led end-to-end product development, design and production functions with a team of five.
- Located and attended niche trade shows in Los Angeles and New York to generate sales and press.
- Praised by Editor In Chief and Fashion Director of VOGUE for being "fresh and original" at debut show in 2009.
- Increased IMU by 14% to LY by negotiating sample and production costs based on meticulous dissection of garment construction.
- Sourced new factories and suppliers for improved pricing creating better margins and profitability.
- Improved production lead-time from 13 weeks LY to 10.5 weeks TY by establishing aggressive deadlines.
- Managed overseas production and imports ensuring timelines were generously met.
- Conducted fit sessions, developed tech packs, vigorously audited samples received and communicated clear changes to meet high standards.
- Directed design production activities and executed T&A calendar with meeting stated milestones and dates.

APPENDIX 1

SAMPLE RESUME #6 - Finance/Accounting
FIRSTNAME LASTNAME
123 Main Street, City, State, Zip
123.567.6789 | prefix@domain.com
linkedin.com/in/firstnamelastname

FINANCIAL AND ACCOUNTING EXPERT

Entrepreneurial Financial Leader with a proven track record of profitable financial management and innovative company development for Fortune 500 firms, progressive small businesses and mid-sized firms. Versatile manager with a diverse combination of financial, operational and technological knowledge and expertise. Possess comprehensive product experience and regulation knowledge for a variety of financial and non-financial products. Particularly skilled in process re-design, workflow analysis, controls, restructuring and change management.

- Strategic Financial & Accounting Management
- Financial System Assessment & Conversions
- Global Chief Financial Officer Experience
- Change Management – Mergers & Acquisitions
- Regulatory, Governance, & Internal Audit
- Leadership and Team Development
- Budgeting, Forecasting, Strategy & Planning
- Operations and Financial Analysis

Accounting Advisory Firm, New York, NY   April 2017 – Present
Founder & Lead Accountant
- Partner with small business owners with capitalizations from up to $450,000 within a variety of industries at a various business growth stages to outline financial plans that support business goals and funding initiatives.
- Establish accounting and bookkeeping operations for remote maintenance and upkeep.
- Make recommendations to ensure clients are compliant to tax filing and accounting regulations.
- Advise clients on created business and financial plans and guide them through the financing or investment process if seeking outside funding to support business initiatives.
- Perform business development activities and client service to ensure satisfaction and referral business.

Global Financial & HR Services Firm, New York, NY   February 2012 – April 2017
Chief Financial Officer
- Maintained staff of 50 handling general ledger, reporting, accounting operations, planning, analysis, forecasting, budgeting, risk management and revenue billing for this division with $260 million in Sales.
- Led a team to uncover a potential loss of over $30 million in cash within nine months.
- Integrated HR related consulting, benefit products and outsourcing revenue into one function, including divisional 10K, 10Q submissions and FX conversions, consolidations and eliminations reporting.
- Directed team in conversions of PeopleSoft to GEAC, Hyperion to INEA; also from GEAC to JD Edwards/
- Monitored accounting for several acquisitions, dissolutions, discontinued operations and mergers.
- Fully coordinated Sarbanes Oxley implementation, developed controls, compliance, remediation.
- Performed due diligence for sale of consulting and outsourcing functions to ultimately divest businesses.
- Reduced redundant processes and staff, increased automation and redesigned process flows to streamline Finance functions. Researched and handled offshore initiatives, product profitability and unit cost studies.

Global Financial Firm (acquired US Firm), Chicago, IL   April 2010 – February 2012
Controller
- Managed staff of 25 performing operational accounting for accounts valued at over $250,000,000 in assets.
- Consolidated post merger processes and designed abandoned property process that allowed the process to be completed within a 2-week period versus a 4.5-week period before the plan implementation.
- Automated financial statement reporting which eliminated 4 positions, saving $350,000 in compensation.

APPENDIX 1

FIRSTNAME LASTNAME – page 2   123.567.6789 | prefix@domain.com

---

Regional CPA Firm, New York, NY   December 2008 – April 2010
Senior Audit Manager
- Specialized in auditing and consulting for financial services, i.e. brokerage, hedge funds and REITs for the corporate client, American Express.
- Produced analyses and financial statements to support audits and handled regulatory reporting.

Charles Schwab & Co, Boston, MA   July 2006 – December 2008
Director, Internal Control &Asset Reconciliation
- Managed 20 staff analyzing internal controls, stock record reconciliations, cash journals and other systems.
- Created internal control procedures for the Risk and Credit services division.
- Assisted in pricing, valuation and reporting functions and audit processes.
- Improved compliance with SEC and NYSE rules, assisted in 10K and 10Q reporting.
- Performed system analysis, design and implementation and automated reconciliations and reporting.

Fidelity Investments, Boston MA
Manager, Customer Tax Reporting   August 2001–July 2006
Senior Analyst, Regulatory and Financial Control

Goldman Sachs, New York, NY   May 1998 – August 2001
Financial Analyst

Deloitte & Touche, New York, NY   December 1995 – April 1998
Senior Auditor

EDUCATION
- MBA - Rutgers University Graduate School of Management, Newark, NJ
- BA - Douglass College, New Brunswick, NJ, Major: Economics/Accounting

CERTIFICATIONS & LICENSES
- Certified Public Accountant, State of NY
- Financial Industry Regulatory Authority (FINRA), Series 7, 63, 27 completed

---

TECHNICAL SKILLS

- ***Desktop Software:*** Microsoft Products – Excel, Access, Word, Project; Lotus Notes, Visio and ABC Flowchart

- ***Relational Databases and Reporting Systems:*** SAP GL, Oracle/PeopleSoft (General, Accounts Payables, Accounts Receivables, Project, Billing, Payroll and Procurement Modules), GEAC, Hyperion, McCormick & Dodge, Collier Jackson, INEA, Lawson Billing, AMB General Ledger, and QuickBooks

- ***Operating Systems:*** ADP, SunGuard, Autocage, SmartSeg, Checkfree, SSC/Camra Trading System

APPENDIX 1

SAMPLE RESUME #7 – Sales Manager in the Pharmaceutical Industry

FirstName LastName
123 Main Street, City, State, Zip
123.567.6789 | prefix@domain.com

BUSINESS RELATIONS & SALES MANAGEMENT LEADER

Building High-Performing Teams to Drive Revenues for New & Repositioned Business Divisions

Agile Market Strategy Executive with proven experience in identifying, analyzing and exploiting market opportunities within various organizational structures and development stages. Results-driven business partner and team builder with demonstrated, repeat success in developing successful teams and organizations. Creative and multi-disciplinary executive renowned for identifying cryptic connections among players from various environments using multi- and cross-disciplinary approaches to deliver innovative solutions. Proven leader with outstanding relationship building skills, strong communication abilities and exceptional emotional intelligence that excels in matrix and hierarchical structures.

- Business, Marketing & Product Branding Strategy
- Plan Formulation & Results-Generating Execution
- Change Management & Resource Allocation
- Quality Control, Process Audit & Logistics
- Distribution Channel & Client Relations
- Business Trend Identification & Forecasting
- Talent & Performance Management
- Fiscal Accountability & Goal Achievement

ARMSTRONG THERAPEUTICS, INC., Baltimore, MD   2011 – present
A biotechnology firm specializing in emerging neurological therapies for nervous system disorders with a $1.4 Billion market capitalization.
Area Relations Director (October 2015 – present)
- Appointed to create a new position to grow select regional accounts using customized business solutions in managed care, specialty pharmacy distribution, marketing, legal and sales management areas to improve service delivery.
- Lead efforts to expand effectiveness of message within the healthcare practitioner community, key industry organizations, internal corporate audiences, government agencies, insurance companies and non-profits.
- Anticipate trends and remain abreast of current scientific and industry knowledge to formulate strategies and implement plans creating opportunity, capitalizing on market shifts and driving market penetration.

Regional Business Manager (October 2011 – October 2015)
- Grew entire business unit's average dollar volume of sales 326%.
- Selected by leadership and peer group to spearhead key corporate projects, such as developing departmental performance metrics, devising customer relationship management systems and introducing a values program.
- Received the Winners Circle Award for expanding the top-ranked business unit by 26% in US Sales in 2010 and placing first in sales among Area Business Managers.
- Awarded #1 Area Business Manager, National Highest Capsule Dollar Volume and National Highest Market Share Awards in 2009 and exceeded $4.4 MM in US sales during this economically challenged period.
- Exceeded goal by 16% achieving top ranked business unit in Eastern region in (108% of goal) for 2010 and 2011.

EMECLEX, INC., Charlotte, NC   2006 – 2011
A start-up, privately owned, medical software technology company developing clinical trial development solutions.
Manager, Business Development
- Cultivated marketing strategy and identified best use of human capital resources to deliver customized solutions.
- Successfully generated company's first sale valued at $50,000 within six months of launch.
- Built a pipeline exceeding $7 MM in premier medical centers and government agencies within first year.

APPENDIX 1

FirstName LastName – page 2   123.567.6789 | prefix@domain.com

IMMUNIMED, INC., Reston, VA   2001 – 2006
A start-up Biotechnology firm specializing in Infectious Disease therapies acquired by TetraNyma in 2006 for $14.4 Billion.
Senior Clinical Marketing Manager
- Pioneered the launch of three novel drugs utilizing entrepreneurial business development and built a top-performing interdisciplinary team consisting of multiple divisions and co-marketing partners.
- Devised a traditional and social marketing strategy to expand current customer base. Managed team effectively by instilling a diagnostic approach to fiscal and business management that prompted appropriate solution development.
- Led nation in exemplary payer relations and policies for managed markets and government affairs.
- Ranked in the top three of forty business units in combined sales each year from 2001 to 2006.
- Generated $27MM of company's $600MM gross sales in 2003 (over 4% of gross revenues for company).
- Drove the business unit growth rate to exceed 25% annually for nine years.
- Received the following awards during tenure:
    - Outstanding Sales Achievement Awards (2002-2006)
    - Chairman's Award (2005)
    - Region of the Year Award (2001-2004)
- Attained Medicaid guidelines for first of class drug, which eventually became national standard for the firm.
- Facilitated public policy changes in Virginia and North Carolina resulting in 10% decrease in infant infection rates.
- Created Infant Wellness Program/Public Health Initiative that was adopted by 72 pediatric centers nationally.
- Established globally recognized program with Johns Hopkins Comprehensive Transplant Center.

HEALTHSAGE, INC., Washington, DC   1997 – 2000
A multi-divisional medical device manufacturer that has currently grown to 11,000 employees and offices in 90 countries.
Senior Sales Representative
- Launched new combined division while restructuring existing product line that generated $17 MM in sales annually.
- Exceeded 100% to goal in product categories annually. Rose from 28th to 7th out of 30 in nine months in first year.
- Developed focused business plan aimed at hospital accounts and distributor relationships; created strategic relationships with targeted health care systems and negotiated comprehensive contracts.

EDUCATION
KELLOGG SCHOOL OF BUSINESS, NORTHWESTERN UNIVERSITY, Evanston, IL, MBA
UNIVERSITY OF KENTUCKY, Lexington, KY, BS - Major: Interior Design & Architecture, Minor: Business

PROFESSIONAL MEMBERSHIPS/ACTIVITIES
Health Care Businesswoman's Association   2009 – Present

National Multiple Sclerosis Society   2006 – Present
- Volunteer/Team Captain for annual MS Walk events

SKILLS
Microsoft Office: Word, Excel, Access, PowerPoint and Outlook; CRM Systems; Proprietary Drug Distribution Systems

APPENDIX 1

SAMPLE RESUME #8 - Retail / Procurement / Construction

FirstName LastName
123 Main Street, City, State, Zip
123.567.6789 | prefix@domain.com
linkedin.com/in/firstnamelastname

RETAIL PROCUREMENT MANAGER

Construction Management | Project Management | Visual Merchandising | Vendor Relations & Selection

NATIONAL RETAILER, New York, NY   July 2016 – January 2018
Senior Sourcing Manager
- Supported four divisions through Centralized Procurement Department of leading women's clothing company.
- Responsible for the procurement and financial account management of over $40 Million in fixtures/furnishings, mannequins, signage, and construction materials used to build and renovate over 150 store projects annually.
- Streamlined vendor responses for RFP review and vendor negotiations by 25% by automating select processes.
- Reduced fixture expenses by 25% across in a market where there was an increase in the cost of commodities.
- Visited vendor manufacturing plants and new store construction sites to verify quality of fixtures and materials.
- Continually value engineered fixtures, visual components and construction materials to reduce expenses.
- Partnered with cross-functional department leaders to implement best practices to increase productivity.
- Served as a strategic partner in the successful opening new division stores in 2016.
- Managed the daily operations of the department while overseeing seven project managers.

REGIONAL BOUTIQUE RETAILER, Inc., Wayne, NJ   November 2010 – July 2016
Purchasing Manager (October 2013 to July 2016)
- Purchased, bid and maintained inventory levels of all non-merchandise items for the company's 750 stores nationwide, 4 Distribution Centers, Corporate Operations Office and the Canadian Home Office.
- Managed annual expense and capital budgets of more than $93 million.
- Directed the purchasing of all services and material required for the expansion of 93 stores in 2 years, such as general construction, store fixtures and furnishings, lighting, flooring, visual, music and security systems.
- Collaborated with Marketing Department to inventory, distribute and replenish marketing materials.
- Develop an online intranet supply ordering system with the IT department for stores to ensure accuracy in expense and supply distribution. Monitored and audited expense monthly.

Assistant Manager (*November 2010 to October 2013*)
- Managed 24-employee staff and inventory for a $1.5 million dollar store in Southern New Jersey.

NATIONAL TEEN RETAILER, Toms River, NJ   May 2004 – June 2010
Co-Manager
- Managed a $2.5 million dollar store that encompassed scheduling of 38 full-time and part-time employees.
- Assumed role of Visual Merchandising Manager and Scheduling Manager to optimize labor cost and sales
- Trained and educated employees in company policies, procedures and sales strategies

EDUCATION:
Community College, Montclair, NJ - *Associates Degree: Retail Management*   June 1994
SKILLS
Proficient in Word, Excel, PowerPoint, Outlook, Island Pacific, Oracle, SAP, Service Channel, Ariba

APPENDIX 1

SAMPLE RESUME #9 - Operations Management / At-Home Period

FirstName LastName
123 Main Street, City, State, Zip
123.567.6789 | prefix@domain.com

VERSATILE OPERATIONS MANAGER

Profitability-focused Operations Manager with demonstrated abilities turning around troubled business units and building strong, collaborative teams that generate profitable with low turnover. Focused leader who consistently attracts and manages superior talent that provides exceptional account oversight and delivers solutions-focused client service. Analyzes and creates operational processes that optimize revenues, profit margins and labor costs.

- Talent Development & Management
- Profitable Operational Management
- Innovative Approach to Problem-Solving
- Diplomatic Communication Skills
- Departmental Budgeting & Forecasting
- Employee Relations & Team Building

Upscale Resort Complex, Tempe, AZ   7/2010 – present
Full service spa and recreation resort complex with $35 Million in annual revenues, 6 properties and a residential complex which holds hotels which hold 225 condominiums, 225 hotel rooms, a full service spa and indoor/outdoor recreation center
Senior Manager of Guest Sales (03/14-present)
- Facilitate $29 Million in revenues through the effective management of a centralized reservations center handling lodging bookings ($5 Million) and season passes, spa bookings and recreation lessons ($14 Million).
- Manage the $735,000 operational budget for Central Reservations Lodging & Guest Services departments and oversee its two departmental managers and 45 employees
- Successfully transitioned and developed the onsite resort lodging call center from centralized call center in Chicago resulting in increased closed sales rate from 19% to 25% within six months, higher revenues year-on-year since and significantly improved agent product knowledge
- Collaborate with sales executives and marketing team to devise and implement marketing plans and ensure operational workflow is communicated with recreation and spa operations, corporate sales and front office
- Interview, hire and evaluate employees on performance metrics regarding group cohesion, guest services execution, troubleshooting and interdepartmental collaboration
- Start and manage the Loyal Guest program for VIP handling initiatives, generating $500K in revenues in 2015
- Implement and orchestrate the resort-wide program to enhance the first-time resort visitor experience
- Spearhead the Employee Experience Committee to maintain cohesive teams among 370 resort employees
- Rate within the Top 3 of 50 departments in survey as the area where employees want to work for last 5 years

Guest Services Manager (7/09-3/14)
- Successfully managed team of 30 tenured employees in all aspects of delivering the mountain experience
- Surpassed season pass budget during a challenging season
- Created efficiencies in staffing through cross training to reduce and sustain labor budgets

PTO – Lincoln School, Chicago, IL   9/2004 – 5/2010
President –Volunteer (9/04 – 5/06)
- Direct all business dealings, marketing initiatives and fundraising projects for this 726-volunteer member parent-teacher organization that has an operating budget of $87,000 per year

Membership Coordinator – Volunteer (9/02-9/04)
- Launched an innovative membership drive that increased membership by 22% in 2002 and 14% in 2003

Payment Data, Des Plains, IL - *Client Services Manager*   7/1999 - 8/2004

EDUCATION

University of Chicago, Chicago, IL - **MBA** | **Cornell University**, Ithaca, NY - **BS Degree in Political Science**

APPENDIX 1

SAMPLE RESUME #10 - Career Transition / Recent Schooling / Real Estate -> Pharmaceutical Industry

FIRSTNAME LASTNAME
123 Main Street, City, State, Zip
123.567.6789 | prefix@domain.com
linkedin.com/in/firstnamelastname

ENTRY-LEVEL PHARMACEUTICAL SALES REPRESENTATIVE

Budding Pharmaceutical Sales Representative who builds prosperous relationships, exceeds quota expectations and facilitates sales through effective client service. Solid scientific and business educational training coupled with strong communication skills and diplomatic negotiation abilities will enable a smooth transition as a productive sales representative. Possess self-motivation, strong work ethic, competitive drive and collaborative spirit to win.

- *Strategic Business Development Planning*
- *Sales Cycle Implementation & Training*
- *Diplomatic Communications Skills*
- *Prospect Pipeline Management*

- *Consultative Sales & Needs Assessment*
- *High Potential Team Building & Promotion*
- *Performance Development & Management*
- *Sales Metrics Analysis & Forecasting*

Rutgers, The State University Of New Jersey, Newark, NJ January 2011
MASTER OF BUSINESS ADMINISTRATION, *Concentration: Marketing* GPA 3.5

Montclair State University, College of Math and Science, Montclair, NJ January 2003
BACHELOR OF SCIENCE, BIOLOGY, *Cum Laude*

PRIVATE REAL ESTATE MANAGEMENT FIRM INC., Nutley, NJ 2004 – Present
Lease Sales & Recording Specialist
- Form solid working relationships with building owners, landlords and building managers to negotiate favorable leases and amendment terms for 789 national cellular equipment locations
- Established the recording process for the company to track and organize current and completed projects, to keep files current and to reconcile documents.
- Execute leases and amendments between landlords & tenants in a timely and efficient manner.
- Meet and exceed required signing targets and related deadlines pertaining to 75 contracts per year.
- Coordinate design visit schedules for architectural, engineering, and administrative teams.
- Served as the Team Leader to roll out the $125,000.00 Memoranda filing project.
- Establish and maintain relationships with county clerks.
- Finalize/edit all title reports and documents meeting all required deadlines.

FORTUNE 1000 ENERGY FIRM, Union, NJ 2001 – 2004
Office Assistant
- Performed office support for a 34-person marketing department answering a high volume of phone calls, compiling purchase orders for marketing collateral, administer correspondence and produce relevant proposal documents.

SKILLS   MS Office Suite (Word, Excel, Outlook, PowerPoint, Access), Social Media Channels, Google Docs

APPENDIX 1

SAMPLE RESUME #11 - Apparel Executive / Marketing

FirstName LastName
123 Main Street, City, State, Zip
123.456.7891 | prefix@domain.com

FASHION OPERATIONS DIRECTOR

Versatile fashion operations professional well-versed in all logistical aspects of creating, launching, marketing, and distributing clothing lines in high-end, boutique retail outlets. Demonstrated experience shopping European, Asian and US markets for trends, creating women's wear lines, partnering with operational outlets and streamlining distribution/supply chain channels.

- *Project Management*
- *International Operations*
- *Quality Control*
- *Creative Development*
- *Pricing & Negotiations*
- *Business Management*
- *Financial Accountability*
- *Production Management*
- *Retail Merchandising & Sales*

EXPEREINCE

Black Ruby UK Inc., London, England   2008 – present
Black Ruby UK is a partnership that creates and distributes the Sanzie Group women's wear line, which is featured/sold in retail outlets such as Neiman Marcus, Nordstrom's, Thomas Pink, contemporary boutique outlets nationwide and its three Sanzie stores located in Palm Beach, FL-US, London, England, and Monaco.
Operations Manager
- Handle production planning and distribution for a $19 million clothing line with factories in India, China, Indonesia and Dominican Republic. Consistently meet global client timelines for 2 seasonal lines yearly that have 17 and 23 distinct items respectively.
- Shop the markets and attend fabric shows monthly in Europe focusing on fashion forward and alternative markets such as Paris, Bonn, Rome, Florence and Dusseldorf.
- Create boards outlining ideas for designs considering pattern, design, price, fit, color, texture, stitching details for each category and cull down options to ultimately create the line.
- Create private label designs for notable, elite labels like Neiman Marcus, Nordstrom's, and Thomas Pink that have resulted in a $3.4 million in revenues.
- Act as a liaison with production finance team in Florida providing needed financial, order and accounting information and answering inquiries regarding the business.
- Work with financiers and accountants to prepare cost sheets, financial spreadsheets, arrange wires, manage factory capital funds, act as factor liaison between production facility and clients.
- Handle day-to-day accounting and sales commissions paid monthly and provide accountants information needed for general ledger monthly close and financial statement creation.
- Partner with vendors to create packaging and displays. Coordinate logistics and shipping to reduce shipping time by 18% and costs by $35,400.

EDUCATION

Louisiana State University, Bachelor of Science in Clothing and Textiles

SKILLS

Microsoft Word, Microsoft Excel, Blue Cherry, Retail Edge

APPENDIX 1

SAMPLE RESUME #12- Entrepreneur / Operations / Business Development

Firstname Lastname
123 Main Street, City, State, Zip
123.567.6789 | prefix@domain.com
linkedin.com/in/firstnamelastname

ENTREPRENEURIAL BUSINESS DEVELOPMENT & OPERATIONS EXECUTIVE

Resource-optimizing Sales and Operations Leader who turns around troubled operations, generates profits during challenging periods and drives sales above corporate objectives consistently. Client-centric approach to conducting needs analysis and creating actionable solutions to logistics issues. Forward-thinking revenue producer who is laser-focused on client development and expectation fulfillment to foster repeat clients and referrals. Develops high caliber teams that exceed needed results, produce positive environments and uphold corporate policies. An award-winning leader in local community development.

- Strategic Business Development & Execution
- Marketing, Branding & Sales Strategy
- Acquisition & Turnaround Expertise
- Change Management & Talent Development
- Fiscal Accountability, Forecasting & Budgeting
- Profitable Pricing & Risk Assessment
- Quality Control & Effective Cost Containment
- Client Retention & Targeted Prospecting

PRIVATE MANAGEMENT CONSULTING FIRM, Indianapolis, IN   February 2008 – present
Founder of this boutique management consulting firm that caters to clients seeking logistical and distribution consultation.
General Manager
- Grew this Midwest company staff from 12 to 19 individuals and doubled revenues since inception.
- Return a year-on-year return to investors from 7-17% through entire tenure.
- Perform rigorous business development activities and in-person client presentations to key decision makers outlining streamlined distribution solutions to their internal and external logistical issues.
- Lead development team for software and website enhancements that dramatically improve productivity.
- Integrated CRM into our daily service protocol that optimized follow-up client communications..
- Evaluated, selected and manage an outsourced IT managed services firm to resolve issues that reduced administrative time spent by management by 35% and drove profitable activities performance.
- *Honored by the Indianapolis Business Journal for 2008 and 2009 as a Fast 100 Business.*
- *Named the 2010 NFIB Small Business Champion by the American Association of Independent Businesses.*

REGIONAL LOGISTICS AND DELIVERY FIRM, Des Moines, IA   March 2004 – December 2007
Leading full-service courier delivery, logistics and warehouse company, with $4.5 Million in revenues.
General Manager
- Doubled sales growth in < 3 years from 2004 to 2007 and remained profitable on 25% less revenues
- Constructed and developed a full-service 21,000 sq ft warehouse and fulfillment center.
- Spearheaded a 'Just in Time Inventory Placement Program' and implemented with national client base.
- Created a division to handle larger national loads which added 22% more in revenues the last 2 years.
- Deployed national transportation service offering weekly ground services in 22+ major markets.

APPENDIX 1

Firstname Lastname– page 2   123.567.6789 | prefix@domain.com

GLOBAL RECRUITMENT FIRM, Chicago, IL.   August 2000 – January 2004
Senior Account Manager
- Performed sales development that produced $25,000 in weekly profits from landing 45-55 new accounts per year and expanding business within legacy accounts for this national accounting recruitment firm.
- Led sales efforts for the Chicago office and received numerous accolades periodic sales leader and margin leader. Heavily contributed to Chicago being the lead office of 13 domestic locations.
- Marketed and positioned accounting and finance staffing services to targeted human resources and financial management prospects through cold calling, networking and referral generation.

INDUSTRY & COMMUNITY LEADERSHIP

Indianapolis Chamber of Commerce, *Membership Chairperson*   2008 – present
- Initiated membership recruitment drives that added 75 members in 2009 and 162 members in 2010.
- Coordinated with Committee Leaders to devise a branded marketing program to improve the image of the Chamber in the local community.

Midwest Management Consultants Association, *Founder*   2007 – present
- Current Board Member and Legislative Committee Chairperson
- Coordinate legislative affairs and work directly with lobbyists and coalition partners.

National Federation of Independent Business   2003 – present
- Named the 2010 NFIB Small Business Champion-Texas by the National Federation of Independent Business.

Soccer Coach – Grade Levels 1st to 4th Grade Girls   2008 – present

EDUCATION

Notre Dame University, Notre Dame, IN   August 2000
Bachelor of Arts in Speech Communication

SKILLS

Microsoft Office (Word, Excel, Outlook, PowerPoint), Salesforce.com CRM

APPENDIX 2
ACTION VERB GUIDE

Use action verbs to tell your story with impact. They let you create impactful bullets that communicate clearly to hiring managers and resume readers exactly what you did and how you did it. Pulled from the resumes and profiles created by Chameleon Resumes for our clients, the list overleaf will help you create your own successful resume.

Remember: Use present tense verbs with current positions and past tense verbs for previous roles.

APPENDIX 2

- Tripled
- Grew
- Returned
- Constructed
- Spearheaded
- Led
- Integrated
- Reduced
- Served
- Evaluated
- Assessed
- Directed
- Managed
- Selected
- Compiled
- Presented
- Built
- Ensured
- Created
- Deployed
- Honored
- Named
- Marketed
- Sold
- Positioned
- Branded
- Communicated
- Drafted
- Consolidated
- Cultivated
- Volunteered
- Tested
- Contributed
- Collaborated
- Partnered
- Initiated

- Implemented
- Devised
- Doubled
- Designed
- Forecasted
- Tracked
- Hired
- Screened
- Supervised
- Inspected
- Strategized
- Supported
- Approved
- Organized
- Procured
- Researched
- Standardized
- Sourced
- Represented
- Processed
- Coordinated
- Orchestrated
- Oversaw
- Advised
- Played
- Interfaced
- Added
- Generated
- Produced
- Founded
- Received
- Restructured
- Structured
- Rebuilt
- Liaised
- Coached

- Consulted
- Executed
- Centralized
- Transitioned
- Moved
- Participated
- Discovered
- Introduced
- Investigated
- Conducted
- Assembled
- Authored
- Wrote
- Reported
- Facilitated
- Mediated
- Monitored
- Presided
- Qualified
- Moderated
- Promoted
- Performed
- Gathered
- Expanded
- Invited
- Arranged
- Crafted
- Prepared
- Recruited
- Prepared
- Testified
- Optimized
- Maximized
- Minimized
- Opened
- Helped

- Recalibrated
- Pitched
- Presented
- Achieved
- Accomplished
- Increased
- Decreased
- Established
- Shifted
- Fostered
- Maintained
- Forged
- Chosen
- Repositioned
- Conceptualized
- Formulated
- Utilized
- Engineered
- Conceived
- Streamlined
- Counseled
- Outperformed
- Planned
- Administered
- Saved
- Exceeded
- Launched
- Negotiated
- Focused
- Cited
- Briefed
- Appointed
- Manifested

ABOUT THE AUTHOR

Lisa Rangel is the founder and managing director of Chameleon Resumes, named a Forbes Top 100 Career Website. She was a moderator of LinkedIn premium groups and career blogger for 8 years. As a recruitment professional for 13 years and as a Cornell University graduate, Lisa has held management and producer roles in numerous companies, ranging from international recruitment conglomerates to focused executive search firms.

In Chameleon Resumes, she has assembled the best team of resume writers and job search consultants who all have prior search firm and corporate recruiting experience—Chameleon is the only firm of its kind! Lisa and her team know first hand which resumes get a response. They've reviewed thousands of resumes over the years and helped top recruiters and talent for top organizations, working with clients in 88 countries.

Lisa is a member of the National Resume Writers' Association and Professional Association of Resume Writers and Career Coaches. She has been featured in person, online and in print on Fast Company, Forbes, LinkedIn, Newsweek, Money, Business Insider, CNBC, BBC, Crain's New York, Chicago Tribune, CIO Magazine, American Marketing Association, eFinancial Careers, The Vault, Monster, U.S. News & World Report, Good Morning America, Fox Business News and many other reputable publications.

She is the author of nine books, creator of the Get Hired Fast job-landing training series at JobLandingAcademy.com, and a serial advice giver through her website ChameleonResumes.com. You can sign up to get advice from Lisa directly into your inbox from:

https://chameleonresumes.com/get-daily-career-tips/

in linkedin.com/in/lisarangel

ALSO BY LISA RANGEL

The Job Landing Mindset

The 6-Figure Resume

Cover Letter E-Notes: The Modern Way to Land Interviews

www.ingramcontent.com/pod-product-compliance
Lightning Source LLC
Chambersburg PA
CBHW030548100526
44583CB00033B/869